P9-CFZ-124

TWENTIETH CENTURY
INTERPRETATIONS
MAYNARD MACK, *Series Editor*
Yale University

NOW AVAILABLE
Collections of Critical Essays
ON

ADVENTURES OF HUCKLEBERRY FINN
ALL FOR LOVE
ARROWSMITH
AS YOU LIKE IT
THE BOOK OF JOB
THE DUCHESS OF MALFI
THE FROGS
SIR GAWAIN AND THE GREEN KNIGHT
THE GREAT GATSBY
GULLIVER'S TRAVELS
HAMLET
HENRY IV, PART TWO
HENRY V
THE ICEMAN COMETH
THE PORTRAIT OF A LADY
SAMSON AGONISTES
THE SCARLET LETTER
THE SOUND AND THE FURY
TOM JONES
TWELFTH NIGHT
UTOPIA
WALDEN
THE WASTE LAND

TWENTIETH CENTURY INTERPRETATIONS
OF

HENRY IV
PART TWO

TWENTIETH CENTURY INTERPRETATIONS
OF

HENRY IV
PART TWO

A Collection of Critical Essays

Edited by

DAVID P. YOUNG

Prentice-Hall, Inc.  A SPECTRUM BOOK *Englewood Cliffs, N. J.*

75235

Contents

TWENTIETH CENTURY INTERPRETATIONS
OF
HENRY IV
PART TWO

Introduction

by David P. Young

There are a number of ways by which one may "place" *Henry IV,
Part Two* as a preliminary to discussion. It is usually thought to be the
sixteenth play in Shakespeare's canon. Thus it comes about midway
in his total *oeuvre* and belongs, most certainly, to his artistic maturity.
The date of composition is interesting to consider as well. It belongs
to the late 1590's—informed conjecture puts it in 1597–98—and thus to
what is probably the richest decade (1595–1605) in the history of the
English theater, as well as to that part of Shakespeare's career in which
he seems to have enjoyed his fullest success as a dramatist on the London stage. At the height of his powers he enjoyed a set of circumstances
—an admiring, attentive public, a competent and close-knit company
of actors, no serious or damaging rivals, and a freedom from restrictive
conventions that allowed him wide experimentation—which he was
able to exploit to the fullest.

With this background in mind, we may inquire about the genre of
this play and its relation to other works by Shakespeare. *Henry IV,
Part Two* is a history play, which means, in terms of Shakespeare's
practice, that it deals with English history as reported in the chronicles
and concerns itself with events and issues pertaining to the reign of
an English king. An element of spectacle inevitably accompanies such
a subject, and for a long time it was felt to be the severe limitation of
the history plays that they dealt in pageantry and catered to a crude
patriotism in their audience. We have gradually come to think otherwise, to see that the histories, like Shakespeare's other plays, are about
individual lives and feelings, and that the tracing of the interpenetra-
tion between public and private, general and particular, impersonal
forces and personal fates, is as rich and subtle as Shakespeare's work
in more familiar genres. The revival of interest in the histories in this
century has been rewarding both on the stage and in the study.

The relation of *2 Henry IV* to the other history plays is complex and
interesting. It is one of a group of eight histories that Shakespeare
wrote during the first half of his career, a linked sequence of dramas
that covers English history from the reign of Richard II (1377–99) to
the accession of Henry VII (1485). In that group of eight it stands third

in the order of historical chronology, but seventh in order of composition, as Shakespeare wrote the tetralogy covering the earlier period, from Richard II to Henry V, some years after his composition of the three Henry VI plays and *Richard III.*

Part Two is most frequently discussed, however, not as a member of an "octology" or a tetralogy, but in relation to its immediate predecessor, *Henry IV, Part One.* While this seems natural enough—it is, after all, the second half of a two-part play—it has in practice been a source of difficulty in seeing the play clearly. For 2 *Henry IV* has always had to stand in the shadow of one of Shakespeare's acknowledged masterpieces, under the obloquy and suspicion that customarily attach to "sequels." Shakespeare, the argument runs, wrote it to capitalize on the success of *Part One,* particularly the popularity of Falstaff; since his motives were mercenary, he had nothing in particular to "say," with the result that the play is merely a weak rehash of the materials so successfully treated in the original. Despite a widely held and convincingly argued modern view that Shakespeare planned both parts together and indeed viewed them as an integral middle section to his tetralogy, the earlier version of *Part Two*'s ill repute is still very much in evidence; it was possible, as recently as 1953, for a reputable critic to speak of the play as "that ramshackle rag-bag of a piece," which "has pot-boiler written all over it." [1]

Is this a just evaluation of the play? Or do we have in *Part Two,* as some would claim, Shakespeare's reassessment of the world he had presented in *Part One,* and thus a play which is more searching than, even in some respects superior to, its predecessor? The way to answer such questions is to view the play not merely as a sequel but as a full-fledged member of the canon and a separate and unified work of art. Surely it deserves such attention, and it must stand up to such treatment if it is ever to rival *Part One* in our esteem. The purpose of this collection of essays, then, has been less to explore the questions of composition raised by the problematic relation between the two parts of *Henry IV* than to analyze *Part Two* in and of itself, in order to discover whether its traditional weaknesses might not, in fact, constitute its peculiar strengths.

Critics of the play, it seems to me, have sometimes involved themselves in contradiction by arguing, on the one hand, that Shakespeare was merely rehashing *Part One* and by complaining, on the other, that there is in the play a disturbing change of tone and, particularly, a loss of the "resilience and breezy opportunism" [2] that characterized Falstaff earlier on. But you cannot have it both ways. If there is a dif-

[1] Richard David, "Shakespeare's History Plays—Epic or Drama?," *Shakespeare Survey 6* (New York and London: Cambridge University Press, 1953), p. 37.
[2] *Ibid.,* p. 38.

ferent tone and a new attitude toward Falstaff, then the play is better described as a deliberate reviewing and re-thinking of the world and characters of *Part One* than as a potboiler. Such a recognition, moreover, is consonant with the practice of Elizabethan dramatists in general and of Shakespeare in particular; both *Hamlet* and *Lear,* for example, are re-visions, second looks at earlier plays probably well known to their audiences. And the two parts of Marlowe's *Tamburlaine* constitute an interesting precedent to the Henry IV plays, at least for those who do not succumb to the potboiler theory in that case too.[3]

1 Henry IV is, after all, a pretty sunny affair; it has some of the finest comic scenes Shakespeare ever wrote; it has an admirable symmetry and develops a rich counterpoint of characters and worlds; and the impression it leaves on the reader or viewer is that of harmony and resolution at every point. One has to search hard and with unusual hindsight to find discords or dissonances in its superb orchestration. That its qualities are those of great art is not to be disputed. But that its geniality and balance do not allow it to pose certain hard questions about the price of involvement in historical processes and political enterprises is also worth noting. Even those characters who are destroyed do not seem to us to have suffered inappropriately; Hotspur is robbed (but his use of that key verb tends to brush past without our notice) of his youth, but not of his gallantry or any of the other qualities that have made him so attractive to us; his death is touching but not tragic. And Falstaff, with an appropriateness we do not question, is allowed his comic resurrection, demonstrating a durability that in no way seems ominous at the time. Likewise, Hal slips neatly and with apparent effortlessness out of his role as wastrel and into his father's favor and the pattern of an ideal prince.

Given these facts, we can perhaps see more clearly why the next appropriate dramatic step might seem to Shakespeare to be a *peripeteia,* why he might want to pose something like the following question: Is there no more cost to these engagements with the "revolution of the times" than a glorious death in battle for rebels like Hotspur (or a pardon for those like Douglas), royal toleration for Falstaff, a quickly and cleanly paid score for the Prince, and a happy old age for Henry? If Shakespeare had ignored this question and pushed straight on to the glories of *Henry V,* we should not have had the penetrating and often discomfiting gaze at political realities and human sacrifice to larger forces that *2 Henry IV* affords us, nor would the great tetralogy have had its careful balance between the essentially negative and costly worlds of *Richard II* and *2 Henry IV* and the largely positive and re-

[3] See G. K. Hunter, "*Henry IV* and the Elizabethan Two-Part Play," *Review of English Studies,* n.s. V (1954), 236–48.

warding circumstances of *1 Henry IV* and *Henry V*. It is by recognizing its essential and somewhat one-sided part in Shakespeare's vision
of the rhythms of history that we can begin to see *Part Two* clearly.
It is, to borrow from Henry's pessimistic speech (at III.i.45ff.), a long
drink from the cup of alteration and a hard look at the book of fate;
and it is on those terms, rather than as an attempt to cash in on Falstaff's popularity, that we can best evaluate it.

Shakespeare takes considerable trouble to warn his audience of the
reversal he has engineered by the (for him) rare device of a prologue.
In one sense Rumour's speech resembles that of the armed prologue
who introduces us to the world of *Troilus and Cressida,* warning us
harshly of the harshness to come; in another sense, since it comes in
the middle of a two-part play, it resembles the chorus of Time in *The
Winter's Tale,* who steps in midway in the action, not only to warn us
of a lapse of sixteen years, but to signal a shift from one mode to another and to invite us to a larger perspective on the events we have
witnessed and are about to witness. Rumour makes no attempt to win
us by graciousness. He is not only blunt and peremptory ("Open your
ears" are his first words); he is sarcastic at the expense of his auditors
("for which of you will stop / The vent of hearing when loud Rumour
speaks?") and deliberately links the ignorance and fickleness of Henry's
subjects ("the blunt monster with uncounted heads, / The still-discordant wavering multitude") to the habits of the audience before him:

> But what need I thus
> My well-known body to anatomize
> Among my household?
>
> (Ind. 20–22)

Whether we like it or not, we have been moved into a world of "smooth
comforts false, worse than true wrongs," from "that royal field of
Shrewsbury" to "this worm-eaten hold of ragged stone, / Where Hotspur's father, old Northumberland, / Lies crafty-sick." The posts bringing false news "come tiring on."

From the vantage point where Rumour has placed us, there now
spreads out rapidly before us a world dominated by misapprehension,
mutability, sickness and decay—side-effects, it would appear, of a period
of political transition. It is the grief-stricken Northumberland who
senses this most clearly in the opening scene and who continues the
choric line begun in the prologue:

> What news, Lord Bardolph? Every minute now
> Should be the father of some stratagem.
> The times are wild; contention, like a horse

> Full of high feeding, madly hath broke loose,
> And bears down all before him.
> (I.i.7–11)

He knows better than to trust the tongue[4] that brings good news, and, when he has heard the truth about the battle at Shrewsbury, compares himself to a deranged fever patient breaking loose from his keeper, and issues his eloquent summons to disorder and destruction. The scene closes with fresh plotting and the news that the Archbishop of York, "Suppos'd sincere and holy in his thoughts," is turning insurrection to religion to save "a bleeding land, / Gasping for life under great Bolingbroke" (I.i.200–208).

Falstaff reiterates these themes in comic fashion in the scene that follows, and we are made particularly aware, in a fashion that does not resemble any treatment of him in *Part One,* of his age, ill-health, and endemic opposition to law and order as embodied in the impressive person of the Chief Justice. There are also hints of vanity and malice in his character which *Part One* did not really touch on but which *Part Two* shows itself willing to explore. This is not to claim that Falstaff has suddenly emerged as an evil person, or even that he is greatly changed from his characterization in *Part One*; it is simply to note adjustments and new emphases which put him in accord with the darker world of this play and its stress on the costliness of temporal existence and political change. The scene ends with a particularly unsuccessful and laborious attempt at humor on Falstaff's part, more peevish than witty, as if to underline the fact that he needs the right audience and favorable circumstances to work his famous magic. The special status which protected him from failure or criticism in his first play seems to be dropping away.

We do not meet Prince Hal until the second act, or the King until the third, but both, when encountered, seem to be suffering from the *malaise* which envelops the play. Hal's first words are an expression of weariness. Through his backchat with Poins runs a dual concern about his father's ill-health and his own failure to achieve consistent princeliness. This latter leads him to needle Poins in a fashion that is not especially attractive. The self-confidence that buoyed him up in the

---

[4] That word, picked up from Rumour's costume, reverberates through the opening scene (e.g., at 69, 74, 84, 97, 101), and recurs in interesting contexts throughout the play, as in Warwick's "The Prince but studies his companions / Like a strange tongue" (IV.iv.68–69); Falstaff's "I have a whole school of tongues in this belly of mine, and not a tongue of them all speaks any other word but my name" (IV.iii.18–20); and the Epilogue's "If my tongue cannot entreat you to acquit me, will you command me to use my legs" (18–19) and "My tongue is weary; when my legs are too, I will bid you good night" (32–34). [Quotations from the play are based on A. R. Humphreys's New Arden Edition (London: Methuen & Co., Ltd., 1966)].

tavern and on the battlefield in *Part One* has, at least temporarily, deserted him. He feels the need to protest that his appearance is deceptive ("Let the end try the man"), and when he undertakes another tavern trick, that of spying on Falstaff, it is with a further emphasis on his sense of degradation and a mocking platitude:

> From a prince to a prentice? A low transformation! that shall be mine,
> for in everything the purpose must weigh with the folly.
>
> (II.ii.167–69)

Most characteristic of his earlier self here is the sense of objectivity about his own actions; a moment earlier he has said:

> Well, thus we play the fools with the time, and the spirits of the wise
> sit in the clouds and mock us.
>
> (134–35)

Hal is biding his time until he is called to the kingship, and the interim does not call for continual merrymaking. He cuts the tavern scene short with impatience and perhaps some relief when Peto arrives with news of the king and the insurrection. His curt "Falstaff, good night," is his last word (cf. "I will now take my leave of these six dry, round, old, withered knights" at II.iv.6–8) to Sir John until the rejection scene.

It is the old king, however, who is made, most appropriately, the central spokesman for the sense of corruption and loss that so distinguishes the atmosphere of the play and overtakes so many of its characters. Even before his late entrance in III.i, we have been made aware that his failing health is emblematic of the state of his kingdom, both for his enemies and his followers. His utterance, when we first meet him and in the scenes that follow, is simultaneously personal and generalized. His own sleeplessness produces a vision of his kingdom and its subjects, and contrasts the peacefulness of the insignificant citizen to the cares of political office, a theme which his son well understands and will reiterate in IV.v, and again in *Henry V*. The magnificent speech about fate is directly based, we learn, on Henry's feelings of betrayal and failure from his own past:

> O God, that one might read the book of fate,
> And see the revolution of the times
> Make mountains level, and the continent,
> Weary of solid firmness, melt itself
> Into the sea, and other times to see
> The beachy girdle of the ocean
> Too wide for Neptune's hips; how chance's mocks
> And changes fill the cup of alteration

With divers liquors? O, if this were seen,
The happiest youth, viewing his progress through,
What perils past, what crosses to ensue,
Would shut the book and sit him down and die.
'Tis not ten years gone,
Since Richard and Northumberland, great friends,
Did feast together, and in two years after
Were they at wars. It is but eight years since,
This Percy was the man nearest my soul.
(III.i.45–61)

While Henry continues to concern himself with the urgent affairs of the present, he is obviously more occupied with the oppression of his past and a pessimistic anxiety about the future, the succession of his son. He clearly does not fully understand Hal, and even his attempts to describe him cheerfully are laced with doubt and distrust:

He hath a tear for pity, and a hand
Open as day for melting charity:
Yet notwithstanding, being incens'd, he's flint,
As humourous as winter, and as sudden
As flaws congealed in the spring of day.
(IV.iv.31–35)

The slightest provocation (e.g., the news that Hal is dining with Poins) is enough to send him into a frenzy of despair:

The blood weeps from my heart when I do shape
In forms imaginary th'unguided days
And rotten times that you shall look upon
When I am sleeping with my ancestors.
(58–61)

So disaster-prone has Henry become that the good news that the rebellion has been put down strikes the final disabling blow of his illness. He recognizes the irony of the circumstance—as Northumberland had earlier in his opposite renewal of strength at disastrous news—and makes of it an occasion for cursing fate:

And wherefore should these good news make me sick?
Will Fortune never come with both hands full,
But write her fair words still in foulest letters?
(102–4)

Right up to the moment of his death and his final full reconciliation with his son, Henry continues to bewail the state of things in his kingdom, to protest the harshness of fate, and to utter dire predictions of the riotous times to come. What saves him from seeming to wallow in self-pity is his genuine concern, above all else, for his kingdom and its subjects, and what keeps him from seeming an isolated and hyperbolic pessimist is the degree to which he seems to express not merely his own fears and doubts, but emotions shared by most of the characters in the play.

To point out the strong choric elements in the play is not, however, to claim that they constitute its full and final insights, its "truth." For the fact is that the sense of fatality and despair so strongly expressed by Henry and others must be linked to the theme of misapprehension introduced at the outset in the person of Rumour. Henry is after all wrong about Hal and wrong about the immediate future, just as so many other characters in the play suffer from some kind of misunderstanding: Falstaff that he will be a royal favorite; Shallow that Falstaff is a person of importance (Shallow also badly misunderstands his past, as Falstaff tells us, but then both he and Falstaff mistake past and future as it turns out; the ability to comprehend time correctly is a test that every character in the play fails at some point); Northumberland that he will be capable of decisive action; the other rebels that they can deal honestly with John of Lancaster; Sir John Colevile that Falstaff is a man of tremendous military prowess; Pistol that he is unusually frightening and eloquent; and the Lord Chief Justice that Hal will mistreat him when he comes to power. Nearly everyone is mistaken about Hal, in a way that makes him central to the focus and movement of the play, and he, who is least mistaken about the state of things, misapprehends the moment of his father's death and precipitates a crisis by taking away the crown.

It is after this honest error that we get the reconciliation between father and son, a powerful scene in itself and a resolution of misunderstanding which sets off a chain reaction of redefinitions and enlightenments. It produces from the old king the most honest statement he has ever made:

> God knows, my son,
> By what by-paths and indirect crook'd ways
> I met this crown, and I myself know well
> How troublesome it sat upon my head.
>   (IV.v.183–86)

And it is for Hal the beginning of a series of actions by which he expresses his understanding of, and readiness for, the difficult role of kingship. He enlightens his brothers, his court, the Chief Justice, and Falstaff and company, and, by implication, all of his new subjects. The final, and most dramatic, of these encounters, the rejection of Falstaff, has claimed an unusually large share of critical interest. Most of the essays in the collection, as well as the excerpts in the *View Points* section, deal with it at one point or another, though none, I hope, too obsessively. My own comments will be brief.

Two intertwined questions are raised by this famous moment: that of Shakespeare's intention, and that of his success in achieving it. In both cases analysis tends to divide its attention between our feelings about Falstaff and our feelings about Hal, or rather Henry V, as he must at this juncture be styled. What the bulk of recent criticism has amply shown, I believe, is that no single emotion or judgment will suffice for either character at this point, and that it is wrongheaded and contrary to the spirit of great drama to call for one. Anyone who has attended to the course of the play must understand that Falstaff has had this coming, that his vanity and misapprehension have brought it about, and that it is in part comic; but these facts do not imply that we must suddenly shut off our sympathy, even our pity, for the man. The other characters in the play—rebels, King, Prince—have shared a melancholy perception of the dangers and privations of political existence, but Falstaff, for all his awareness and superb commentary on the life around him, has never had to admit his own involvement, to acknowledge the contradiction between his wish to be outside of time and social ties, and his hope to profit by them. That he should be brought so abruptly to a knowledge of the facts is something which the course of the play should encourage us to acknowledge both as a necessity and a matter for sympathy and regret.

Hal's case is more similar than one might at first suspect. He too is bound by necessities which do not really serve to make him more heroic or humane. His gesture too, it seems to me, calls more for sympathy than for admiration. I see no reason why we should feel totally comfortable about what he has to do, or why we should think that he does. Is there anything in this play which urges us to feel that the assumption of kingship is without personal cost? Hal speaks most clearly about his understanding of these matters in his soliloquy to the crown:

> O majesty!
> When thou dost pinch thy bearer, thou dost sit
> Like a rich armour worn in heat of day,
> That scald'st with safety.

(IV.v.27–30)

In his public utterances he hints at the same thing. His long friendship with Falstaff he compares to a dream which, being awaked, he must despise, not because it was despicable while it lasted, but because it was an illusion that could not be sustained. Earlier he had said to his brothers and the Chief Justice:

> The tide of blood in me
> Hath proudly flow'd in vanity till now.
> Now doth it turn, and ebb back to the sea,
> Where it shall mingle with the state of floods,
> And flow henceforth in formal majesty.
>
> (V.ii.129–33)

There are implications in this image of a loss of personal identity, forced on the subject by the new role of formal majesty, that rich, pinching armour of the earlier image. If Hal could be, in the earlier play, as madcap Prince of Wales, "of all humours that have showed themselves humours" (*Part One*, II.iv.103), he cannot be so now. He is constrained by his acceptance of his political mask, in much the same way that Falstaff is constrained by his as tutor and feeder of riots. Both men have become, in a sense and for the moment, humour characters. The loss is somehow both more serious and more comic in Falstaff's case, but the similarity is there.

If this resolution involves a kind of narrowing in the personalities and awarenesses ("Make less thy body," Hal has had to tell Falstaff) of the two characters, it does not make a similar demand on us, who remain fortunately free from the political involvements and temporal ravagings of the play. This is the one point on which I find myself in disagreement with C. L. Barber's excellent analysis of *Part Two*. He argues that the rejection calls for "a drastic narrowing of awareness," [5] and that it therefore fails dramatically. But we can distinguish, I think, between characters having to shut off parts of their minds, as Barber puts it, and an audience having to do so. The temptation is great enough, as so many analyses of the play have shown. But I should argue that the challenge of *Part Two* is whether we are able to keep our minds open to everything it offers us, however contradictory or unpleasant. As so often with Shakespeare, it is not so much a question of his success as of ours.

It would not do to conclude a discussion of this play without some attention to the pervasiveness and range of its comedy. If Shakespeare has produced a more somber vision of political change, he has not sacrificed his great comic talent, but rather altered the comic elements of the preceding play to a key that is more bitter and realistic yet hardly less successful. Falstaff, proceeding amiably to his downfall, is still hugely funny, and there surround him, like so many pocked eccentric moons around a great decaying planet, a rich disreputable host of satellite characters—Bardolph, Pistol, Hostess Quickly, Doll Tearsheet, Fang and Snare, Shallow and Silence, and the Gloucestershire recruits —all deployed in the careful counterpoint to the "serious" aspects and

⁵ See below, p. 47.

characters of the play that is so important an aspect of Shakespeare's genius. Pistol, a personal favorite, will serve nicely as an illustration of the way in which Shakespeare's comic energy continues to function. In one sense Pistol has replaced Hotspur in the "huffing part" [6] and the distance between them is a measure of the difference between the respective plays they inhabit: the zest and imagination with which Hotspur did his swaggering, all the charm which oddly linked him with Falstaff, have come down to this ragged creature, strutting and preening, his mouth full of scraps from the playhouse. The preposterous discrepancy between his linguistic pretensions and his actual person links him to the general atmosphere of illusion and the repeated process by which reality intrudes upon subjective visions of grandeur and political power. Pistol's brief moment of glory comes in V.iii, where he bustles into Shallow's orchard, an unwitting Rumour (the news he brings is true, but everyone's inference from it false) to whose style Falstaff must adapt—"O base Assyrian knight, what is thy news? / Let King Cophetua know the truth thereof"—before he can learn what he wants to know. There is, finally, a more than comic significance in Pistol's aping of the bombast and swagger of the Senecan style, which was far enough out of fashion and yet familiar enough to make him especially amusing to contemporary audiences. In that somewhat self-conscious theatrical device lies an analogy, aimed straight at the audience, between illusion and truth in the world of the play on the one hand, and stuffed rhetoric and sober realism in the playhouse on the other. Sections of the audience may have preferred strutting and bellowing tyrants on the stage, but the connection between the blunt facts of political reality and a kind of esthetic truthfulness was there if they cared to look for it. That this issue should be on Shakespeare's mind, especially in light of the fact that he was returning, a little grimly and in an uncompromising spirit, to the materials of an immensely popular play for a second look, should surprise no one. And whether or not Pistol was a source of insight, he seems to have been a resounding success, as is suggested by his sharing feature billing with Falstaff on the title page of the quarto: "The Second part of Henrie the fourth, continuing to his death, and the coronation of Henrie the fift. With the humours of Sir Iohn Falstaffe, and swaggering Pistol." [7]

If we have lost much of the stage business and theatrical context that made Pistol so hilarious to his contemporaries, that is fortunately not

[6] That Hotspur was famous for this quality is indicated by the fact that Rafe, in *The Knight of the Burning Pestle,* asked to show what he can do on stage by speaking "a huffing part," responds with a garbled version of the "By heaven, methinks it were an easy leap" speech from *1 Henry IV* (I.iii.201ff.) .

[7] This is no accident. Pistol is similarly featured, despite relatively minor roles, on the title pages of the quartos of *The Merry Wives of Windsor* and *Henry V.* He was apparently a great favorite.

true of the play he inhabits. Surely it is hardly necessary to stress the interest and appeal that *Henry IV, Part Two* has had, and is likely to continue to have, in this century. Its status as a history play has included it in the marked revival of interest that modern study and production have lavished on that genre. And its relatively grim view of the deceptiveness and costliness of political existence is one which we are ready to understand and acquiesce in. But the point is surely not so much the somewhat subjective discovery that Shakespeare is our contemporary as the more reliable and less narrowing one that we are his, a privilege we share with many other eras and an adequate explanation of the interest, insight, and enthusiasm that plays like this one continue to excite.

PART ONE

Interpretations

Time's Subjects: The Sonnets and King Henry IV, Part II

by L. C. Knights

The Shakespeare of early maturity—the Shakespeare newly emerged from the apprentice period of *Henry VI* and *Titus Andronicus* and *The Taming of the Shrew*—possessed in an eminent degree a quality without which no poet ever wrote poetry. I mean simply an energetic consciousness and an appetite for life: a zest that displayed itself in verbal fluency and virtuosity, a readiness to experiment, a capacity for intellectual excitement, and a lively observation of the varied forms of nature and humanity. This buoyancy is obvious, and without it Shakespeare would not have become the great poet that he is. But buoyancy alone never made a great poet, let alone a great tragic poet. Great poetry demands a willingness to meet, experience and contemplate all that is most deeply disturbing in our common fate. The sense of life's tragic issues comes to different men in different ways. One of the ways in which it came to Shakespeare is not uncommon; it was simply a heightened awareness of what the mere passage of time does to man and all created things. There are many of the Sonnets that show the impact of time and mutability on a nature endowed with an uncommon capacity for delight. And it is surely no accident that one of the first plays in which we recognize the great Shakespeare—the Second Part of *King Henry IV*—is a play of which the controlling theme is time and change. In that play, and in the sonnets on time, we see clearly the beginning of the progress that culminates in *King Lear* and the great tragedies.

1

As everyone knows, the Sonnets contain a number of themes that seem to issue directly from the life history of the poet; and if we make a prose paraphrase of the poems in the order in which they appear in Thorpe's edition of 1609 we can piece together a story that has a tantalizing appearance of fragmentary autobiography. There are various reasons for not finding this an entirely satisfactory procedure. One of them is that it takes no account of the close connexion between technical mastery and the degree of a writer's engagement in what he is writing about. Part of the interest the Sonnets have for us is that in them, within the limitations of a highly conventional form, we can see Shakespeare working towards power and subtlety in the use of language—a process comparable to the development of his dramatic blank verse. But they are comparatively early work and we find within them very different levels of poetic achievement. If we are seeking the themes in which Shakespeare's interests are most deeply engaged, we need to be alert to the varied potency of the language. It is only when we really accept this truism that we are in any position to decide in what ways Shakespeare followed Sidney's injunction—"Fool, said my Muse to me, look in thy heart and write."

It is at all events clear that some, at least, of the sonnets in which the "story" element is intrusive are among the least interesting as poetry. Sonnet XLII, for example ("That thou hast her, it is not all my grief"), which is as explicit as any concerning the mistress stolen by the friend, would very properly have been ignored if it had appeared in an anthology of anonymous verse. But if this ingenious little exercise is considered too artificial even for the purposes of elementary comparison, we may take a sonnet that, with some genuine individuality of phrasing, deals directly with a personal relationship, and put beside it another in which the "personal" theme involves the poet in a meditation of a very different kind. Here, then, is Sonnet CII, which deals with the relationship of poet and patron, followed by Sonnet LX, which is one of many whose ostensible purpose is to promise immortality to the beloved.

> My love is strengthen'd, though more weak in seeming;
> I love not less, though less the show appear:
> That love is merchandiz'd whose rich esteeming
> The owner's tongue doth publish everywhere;
> Our love was new, and then but in the spring,
> When I was wont to greet it with my lays;
> As Philomel in summer's front doth sing,
> And stops her pipe in growth of riper days:
> Not that the summer is less pleasant now
> Than when her mournful hymns did hush the night,
> But that wild music burthens every bough,
> And sweets grown common lose their dear delight.

Therefore, like her, I sometimes hold my tongue,
Because I would not dull you with my song.

Like as the waves make towards the pebbled shore,
So do our minutes hasten to their end;
Each changing place with that which goes before,
In sequent toil all forwards do contend.
Nativity, once in the main of light,
Crawls to maturity, wherewith being crown'd,
Crooked eclipses 'gainst his glory fight,
And Time that gave doth now his gift confound.
Time doth transfix the flourish set on youth
And delves the parallels in beauty's brow,
Feeds on the rarities of nature's truth,
And nothing stands but for his scythe to mow:
    And yet to times in hope my verse shall stand,
    Praising thy worth, despite his cruel hand.

The difference in tone and manner needs no comment. Sonnet CII has, most evidently, "the delight in richness and sweetness of sound" which Coleridge noted as one of the signs of original genius in a young poet. It is very beautiful, but the beauty is that of romantic enchantment; it asks an entirely different kind of reading from the other. Sonnet LX is urgent and forthright; there are powerful phrases, but none that tempts us to linger on a beauty that is extrinsic to the matter in hand. Shakespeare, we feel, is fully engaged in the imaginative evocation of the irreversible processes of time. If we were to try to summarize the plain sense of the poem we should have to say something like this: —"Nothing can resist the encroachments of time, which continually takes away what it gives; yet my verse shall continue to exist and to sing your praises to future generations." But in the poetry it is the logically subordinated matter of time's action—vividly realized in the superb imagery of twelve out of the fourteen lines—that enlists our feelings, that we remember, and not the promise at the end. And this is an observation that can be generalized.

It has become a commonplace that one of the most consistently developed themes of Shakespeare's Sonnets—of those at all events in which the linguistic vitality is highest—is Time.[1] Not of course that

---

[1] There are of course others notable as poetry that do not fall within this grouping. Of these some are interesting for the introduction of new tones, notably of a detached irony. I should instance especially some of the "rival poet" group— LXXIX to LXXXVII, for example. Others again express bitterness, protest and self-accusation, with a vigour of phrasing and rhythm which, if it does not always fully define the painful feelings involved, is a clear sign of the breaking through of new insights.

Time's "rage" is always the ostensible or formal subject. It is simply
that whenever there is occasion to mention Time and "nature's changing course" the theme takes possession: there is a sharpness and urgency of phrase; and however fast we hold to the thread of sense and
argument, the imagery involves us in a world where

> everything that grows
> Holds in perfection but a little moment,

where

> men as plants increase,
> Cheered and check'd even by the self-same sky,
> Vaunt in their youthful sap, at height decrease,
> And wear their brave state out of memory,
>   (XV)

where, in short, "nothing stands but for [Time's] scythe to mow." One
reason of course why Time comes into the picture at all is that many
of the sonnets are about ways of defeating him—getting married and
having children, or writing immortal verse, or, best of all, loving so
truly that Time can make no difference. But the poet is not interested
in the young patron's posterity with the same intensity of concern that
is evoked by the signs of beauty's passing (consider, for example, Sonnets V, XII and XV); and even the magnificent assertion of love's in-
dependence of Time in Sonnet CXVI

> —Love's not Time's fool, though rosy lips and cheeks
> Within his bending sickle's compass come—

is (for me) simply an assertion, rather than a final insight to which we
are compelled by that honesty of imagination which takes everything
into account. The imagination of course can leap ahead of experience,
though only in such a way that experience—what is intimately known
—feels itself able to follow in its tracks; and both Sonnet CXVI ("Let
me not to the marriage of true minds") and Sonnet CXXIV ("If my
dear love were but the child of state"), and perhaps others, may be
taken as pointing forward to fundamental recognitions to be found in
Shakespeare's later work. But in the sequence as a whole the assurance
of love's "unknown" worth

> —It is the star to every wandering bark,
> Whose worth's unknown, although his height be taken—
>   (CXVI)

is, as yet, set over against what the imagination has made most real:
there are whole tracts of experience still to be crossed. What we feel,
again and again, in those sonnets that are most powerfully alive, is the

sense of Time—the "dial's shady stealth"—summed up in unforgettable images of the changing seasons and the wasting years.

One may suppose that the early work of genius, where it is most deeply felt, must contain marked premonitions of later development; there is a basic cast of mind and there are fundamental preoccupations. Perhaps in the Sonnets "the essential Shakespeare" is to be found in a fourfold inclination of the spirit. There is a keen and pervasive love of life—especially of all that suggests fresh and unforced latent power, including the world of nature, into which by metaphor and analogy man is so often assimilated. There is an equally keen, equally pervasive feeling for the stealthy and unimpeded undermining by Time of what the heart holds most dear:

> Since brass, nor stone, nor earth, nor boundless sea,
> But sad mortality o'er-sways their power,
> How with this rage shall beauty hold a plea
> Whose action is no stronger than a flower?
>
> (LXV)

And finally, allied with a capacity for self-searching and moral discrimination, there is a groping for some certitude to set over against the perpetual flux of things, an intimation that love alone "stands hugely politic, That it nor grows with heat nor drowns with showers" (CXXIV).

In the Shakespearean progress all these deeply personal leanings will be richly nourished and will unfold into a pattern, a structure of meanings, far more rich and complex than can be found in the Sonnets themselves. There will be an unfailing increase of delighted observation, not only of all that is simply beautiful but, as we should expect from the early plays, of all the varied forms of life: not only of the spring and foison of the year but of every variety of living thing— the peacock that "stalks up and down . . . a stride and a stand," the distracted tavern-keeper "that hath no arithmetic but her brain to set down her reckoning," the vain man who "bites his lip with a politic regard, as who should say, 'There were wit in this head, and 'twould out.' " [2] At the same time, the preoccupation with mutability will become a preoccupation not only with deceitful appearances and false-seeming but with the sources of illusion in the recesses of personal life, in the distorted imagination: a preoccupation leading in recoil to a profound searching for something that, opposed to appearance and in spite of time and death, may be welcomed as reality. And when that

---

[2] That these three bits of observation are recklessly thrown into the passing jest of a satirical knave (*Troilus and Cressida,* III.iii) suggests something of the unfailing Shakespearean abundance.

patient passionate exploration has reached its centre there will be a
marvelous celebration of values that are not only in wish but in fact
"builded far from accident"—values that are first disengaged and established by probing the varied negations of evil and false choice, and
then celebrated more directly in complex dramatic symbols of renewal.
From the Sonnets to *The Tempest* Shakespeare's progress as a dramatist is not to be summed up as a series of adventures of the soul; like
that of all great artists it is a directed exploration. True enough, it is
only when we begin to see the whole pattern that we can realize how
completely Shakespeare was committed, for in each new venture there
is freedom as well as commitment, and nothing could be further than
these plays from the compulsive following of an idea. But the imagination has its responsibilities, and Shakespeare found his when, in a
deeply personal experience, he confronted the power of Time.[3]

[3] In a book on *The Elizabethan Love Sonnets* that appeared after this chapter was
drafted, Mr. J. W. Lever has put forward a well-argued case (pp. 162–272) for finding in Shakespeare's sonnets a significant development, culminating in a genuine
resolution of conflicts springing from a deeply experienced sense of the precariousness of human values in a world where man's faults and Time's power are inescapa-
ble facts. A passionate friendship—in which the Friend is the epitome of beauty
and truth, and the Poet's love for him "the crystallization, in terms of a personal
medium, of the artist's love of life on all the planes of phenomenal being" (p. 187)
—is torn apart by faults on both sides, and the ideal qualities glimpsed in the
Friend are exposed as subject to time and change. It is because the facts are so honestly recognized that the poet is able to disengage from all the relativities of everyday living the one absolute of human experience, which is the transforming power
of love. In the sonnets that Mr. Lever sees as concluding the series a deliberate
survey of the worst that Time can do (e.g., Sonnet LX) leads into a triumphant affirmation of a love which is not subject to his power (Sonnets CXV, CXXIV, CXXV,
CXVI, CVII, LV).

Mr. Lever's chapter contains some of the most intelligent criticism of the Sonnets
that I have seen, and all readers of Shakespeare can learn from it: notably from his
insistence on the way in which the Sonnets are permeated with the great central
concerns of the age (cf. pp. 166–167 and p. 276), from his descriptions of the quasi-
dramatic function of the imagery (p. 168), from his account of the influence—both
pervasive and specific—of the last Book of Ovid's *Metamorphoses* (pp. 248–72 *pas-
sim*), and from some brilliant particular analysis; and even those who do not completely accept his re-ordering of the sequence are likely to agree that he has brought
together many sonnets that are mutually illuminating. But after much pondering I
still feel that the affirmation of love's power—which for Mr. Lever is a triumphant
and grounded assertion of a lived experience—is to some extent *anticipatory*. Mr.
Lever's case, in short, depends on attributing to certain sonnets a depth and range
of significance that I cannot find there. His account of Sonnet LX, "Like as the
waves make toward the pebbled shore" (pp. 252–5) is sensitive criticism of a kind
that makes my own comments on the poem seem very inadequate indeed; yet even
here, it seems to me, the argument is pushed too hard.

> Nativity, once in the main of light,
> Crawls to maturity, wherewith being crown'd,
> Crooked eclipses 'gainst his glory fight,
> And Time that gave doth now his gift confound.

2

In Sonnet LXIV, pondering the general instability of things, Shakespeare had instanced the shifting edges of the sea:

> When I have seen the hungry ocean gain
> Advantage on the kingdom of the shore,
> And the firm soil win of the watery main,
> Increasing store with loss and loss with store . . .

The image is repeated, with an added note of irony for men's expectation of stability, in the Second Part of *King Henry IV*:

> O God! that one might read the book of fate,
> And see the revolution of the times
> Make mountains level, and the continent,
> Weary of solid firmness, melt itself
> Into the sea! and, other times, to see
> The beachy girdle of the ocean
> Too wide for Neptune's hips; how chances mock,
> And changes fill the cup of alteration
> With divers liquors! [4]

Here is indeed "a compound universal metaphor," and Mr. Lever convincingly demonstrates how wide-reaching it is; yet to speak of the first three lines of the quatrain as "an epitome . . . of all Shakespearean tragedies" is, surely, to read into them more than they will bear. Similarly, Sonnet CVII ("Not mine own fears, nor the prophetic soul of the wide world") is said to commemorate "a moment of stillness when all the contradictions of life are suspended in the autumn glow of Love's victory over Time" (p. 267). That, no doubt, is the claim made by the poem itself; but we may still question the justice of the claim:

> Now with the drops of this most balmy time
> My love looks fresh, and Death to me subscribes . . .

Death as it is felt in *Hamlet?* or as when Lear enters with Cordelia dead in his arms? I still feel, in short, that the defiance of Time, though real enough and certainly indicative of the *direction* of growth, cannot be effective until the challenge of negation has been faced more fully and the resolution worked out at even deeper levels. Indeed in *Lear* and the later plays there is no defiance, and the fundamental acceptance of life that they embody is the more assured because, subjected to a keener testing, it takes up into itself doubts and questionings that are all but overwhelming. But *anticipation* of what is still to come there certainly is in the Sonnets (indeed the final resolution might well be described in the strange phrase of Sonnet CVII, "Incertainties now crown themselves assur'd"), and Mr. Lever's account should be read by all who are interested in the nature and direction of the experience that they embody.

⁴ In each instance Shakespeare is drawing on the passage from Book XV of Ovid's *Metamorphoses*, which so haunted his imagination. See Knox Pooler's Arden edition of the Sonnets, p. 66, and, more especially, J. W. Lever, *The Elizabethan Love Sonnets*, pp. 248ff.

This, so far as any one passage can, suggests the nature of the imaginative vision that is now coming to expression in the plays. 2 *Henry IV*, a tragi-comedy of human frailty, is about the varied aspects of mutability—age, disappointment and decay. The theme of "policy" is of course continued from Part I, and sometimes it is presented with similar methods of ironic deflation; but we cannot go far into the play without becoming aware of a change of emphasis and direction, already marked indeed by the words of the dying Hotspur at Shrewsbury,

> But thought's the slave of life, and life time's fool;
> And time, that takes survey of all the world,
> Must have a stop.

Each of the three scenes of the first act gives a particular emphasis to elements present in Part I, though largely subdued there by the brisker tone, by the high-spirited satire. Now the proportions are altered. Act I, scene i is not comic satire: it is a harsh reminder of what is involved in the hard game of power politics—the desperate resolve ("each heart being set / On bloody courses . . .") and the penalties for failure; and for some thirty lines, throughout Northumberland's elaborate rhetoric of protestation against ill news (I.i.67–103), the word "dead" (or "death") tolls with monotonous insistence. Now just as the comedy of the first meeting of the conspirators in Part I was in keeping with the Falstaffian mode that so largely determined the tone of that play, so this scene is attuned to the appearance of a Falstaff who seems, at first perplexingly, to be both the same figure as before and yet another; it is as though we had given a further twist to the screw of our binoculars and a figure that we thought we knew had appeared more sharply defined against a background that he no longer dominated. When Falstaff enters with his page ("Sirrah, you giant, what says the doctor to my water?"), throughout his exchange with the Lord Chief Justice, and in his concluding soliloquy, it is impossible to turn the almost obsessive references to age and disease, as the references to Falstaff's corpulence are turned in Part I, in the directions of comedy.[5] Later, Falstaff will try again his familiar tactics of evasion—"Peace, good Doll! do not speak like a death's-head; do not bid me remember

[5] The Scriptural references in which both parts of this play abound (see Richmond Noble, *Shakespeare's Biblical Knowledge*, pp. 169–81) seem to me to take on a more severe significance in Part II; in the scene under consideration the references to Job, in particular—"and your bodies like the clay" (xiii.12), "his candle shall be put out with him" (xviii.6), and "Among old persons there is wisdom, and in age is understanding" (xii.12)—seem to point a sombre irony. Noble (p. 65 and p. 174) says that 2 *Henry IV* "is the earliest play in which Genevan readings show a decided preponderance over Bishops'," which suggests a comparatively fresh re-reading of considerable parts of the Bible at this time.

mine end" (II.iv.229–30); but from the scene of his first appearance
the well-known *memento mori*, if not—as in *The Revenger's Tragedy*
—actually present on the stage, has certainly been present to the minds
of the audience. "Is not . . . every part about you blasted with an-
tiquity?"—to that question wit in its wantonness must make what reply
it can.

Scene iii, where some of the principal rebels discuss their resources
and prospects, is short but significant. As in the preceding scenes the
significance is found not in any precisely controlled minute particulars
of the poetry but simply in a certain expansiveness and insistence at
key points; what our thoughts are directed towards is the lack of cer-
tainty in human affairs and the consequent precariousness of those
hopes that are so often referred to (seven times in sixty one lines, to be
exact). Hastings is for going ahead and trusting that things will turn
out well; Lord Bardolph urges caution.

> *Hastings.* But, by your leave, it never yet did hurt
> To lay down likelihoods and forms of hope.
> *L. Bardolph.* Yes, if this present quality of war,
> Indeed the instant action, a cause on foot,
> Lives so in hope, as in an early spring
> We see the appearing buds; which to prove fruit,
> Hope gives not so much warrant as despair
> That frosts will bite them.[6]

This is followed by an elaboration of the parable of the man who began to build and, because he had not counted the cost, was not able to
finish (*Luke*, xiv, 28–30):

> Like one that draws the model of a house
> Beyond his power to build it; who, half through,
> Gives o'er and leaves his part-created cost
> A naked subject to the weeping clouds,
> And waste for churlish winter's tyranny.

The Archbishop of York then intervenes on the side of immediate action—

---

[6] The very slight alteration of the Folio punctuation that I have made here seems
to me to give excellent sense to a passage usually labelled corrupt. Lord Bardolph
says, in effect, "Yes, it does do harm if (as in the present case) a military enterprise
relies on hope prematurely aroused, as we see buds appear in a too early spring,
etc." The line "Indeed the instant action, a cause on foot," is emphatic repetition
as Bardolph tries to impress Hastings with his own sense of the desperate importance of seeing their present enterprise as an example of the general rule about
not counting your chickens, etc.

The commonwealth is sick of their own choice;
Their over-greedy love hath surfeited:
An habitation giddy and unsure
Hath he that buildeth on the vulgar heart . . . ,

and it is characteristic of this play that the very fickleness of the common people, dwelt on at some length, should be used to point an obvious moral—"What trust is in these times?"—and, simultaneously, adduced as a ground for optimism. It is the impetuous Hastings who carries his policy and, with unintended irony, hustles off his fellows to try their chance:

We are time's subjects, and time bids be gone.

The world of *King Henry IV, Part II*—the world we are introduced to in the first Act—is a world where men are only too plainly time's subjects, yet persist in planning and contriving and attempting by hook or by crook to further their own interests. Most of them, drawing a model of a desirable future beyond their power to build, are, in the course of the play, disappointed. Since there is no close poetic texture lengthy quotation is unnecessary, but it is worth remarking how often the pattern of hope and disappointment is repeated. Hotspur at Shrewsbury—so we are reminded early in the play—had "lined himself with hope,"

Eating the air on promise of supply,
Flattering himself in project of a power
Much smaller than the smallest of his thoughts.
And so, with great imagination
Proper to madmen, led his powers to death,
And winking leap'd into destruction.
(I.iii.27–33)

The news of Hotspur's death reaches Northumberland hard on the heels of "certain news" ("As good as heart can wish") of rebel victory. In the very scene in which Hotspur's folly is recalled the rebel leaders allow themselves an over-optimistic estimate of their resources, as we see when, before the encounter with the royal forces, Northumberland again defaults, sending "hearty prayers" for their success instead of men: "Thus do the hopes we have in him touch ground" (IV.i.17). When the king's generals offer to negotiate, Hastings (who might indeed adopt Pistol's somewhat travel-stained motto, "Si fortune me tormente, sperato me contento") finds fresh grounds for optimism: "Our peace shall stand as firm as rocky mountains" (IV.i.188)—and on that note the rebel generals walk into the prepared trap. It may of course be said that a play about an unsuccessful rebellion was bound to put

some emphasis on frustrated hopes; but it is not only the Northumberland faction who provide examples of the ironic discrepancy between
what is planned for and what is achieved. Henry Bolingbroke, caught
in the toils of "necessity" (for "to end one doubt by death / Revives
two greater in the heirs of life" [IV.i.199–200]), spends his powers seeking an elusive stability. It is when this is almost achieved, the long-
planned crusade about to be embarked on—"And every thing lies level
to our wish" (IV.iv.7)—that his own strength fails him. The scene in
which he hears of the rebel overthrow is indeed an obvious parallel to
that in which Northumberland declared that ill tidings "have in some
measure made me well" (I.i.139):

> And wherefore should these good news make me sick?
> Will Fortune never come with both hands full,
> But write her fair words still in foulest letters? . . .
> I should rejoice now at this happy news;
> And now my sight fails, and my brain is giddy . . .
> (IV.iv.103–9)

It is of course true that Henry has the satisfaction of a reconciliation
with his eldest son, and dies hoping that the reign of Henry V will be
quieter than his own,

> for what in me was purchased,
> Falls upon thee in a more fairer sort.

But in the imaginative impact of the play as a whole Hal's robust assertion of *de facto* sovereignty

> —My gracious liege,
> You won it [the crown], wore it, kept it, gave it me;
> Then plain and right must my possession be—

count for little beside the bleak and disillusioned summary of his reign
that the elder Henry has just given his son (IV.v.183ff.). As for Falstaff,
there is the superb comedy of the scene where he and his companions
indulge themselves in what, to any sober view, is the most imbecile bit
of wishful thinking that ever deluded poor mortals.

> *Pistol.* Sir John, thy tender lambkin now is king;
>   Harry the fifth's the man . . .
> *Falstaff.* What, is the old king dead?
> *Pistol.* As nail in door: the things I speak are just.
> *Falstaff.* Away, Bardolph! saddle my horse. Master Robert Shallow, choose
>   what office thou wilt in the land, 'tis thine. Pistol! I will double-charge
>   thee with dignities.
> *Bardolph.* O joyful day!

I would not take a knighthood for my fortune.
Pistol. What! I do bring good news.
Falstaff. Carry Master Silence to bed. Master Shallow, my Lord Shallow,
—be what thou wilt; I am Fortune's steward—get on thy boots; we'll
ride all night. O sweet Pistol! Away Bardolph! [*Exit* Bardolph] Come,
Pistol, utter more to me; and withal devise something to do thyself good.
Boot, boot, Master Shallow! I know the young king is sick for me. Let us
take any man's horses; the laws of England are at my commandment.
Blessed are they that have been my friends; and woe to my lord chief
justice!
Pistol. Let vultures vile seize on his lungs also!
"Where is the life that late I led?" say they:
Why, here it is; welcome these pleasant days!

In this context it is plain that the King's mutability speech already
quoted (p. 19, above) is not just a bit of moralizing, appropriate to a
sick and disappointed man. It is not merely "in character"; it is an
explicit formulation of feelings and attitudes deeply embedded in the
play. Act III, the central act, has only two scenes, one at court, one in
Gloucestershire, and the second succeeds the first without a break.
With the King's words still in our ears we are given (among other
things) one of the most superb variations in English literature on the
theme of *le temps perdu*. Act III, scene ii, like the later Cotswold
scenes, is firmly rooted in the actual. Life is going on in this little bit
of rural England, and will go on, for all the wars and civil wars now
and to come—the smith must be paid, the hade land sown with red
wheat, and the well-chain mended.[7] That life is vividly present to us,
built up little by little with unobtrusive art. But the scene is drenched
in memory. In the first fifty lines, as Shallow recalls the poor pranks of
his mad days at Clement's Inn, the exploits of young Jack Falstaff who
is now old, and of old Double who is dead, we are at least as much
aware of the past (and of the fact that it *is* the past) as of anything in
the present. There follows the arrival of Bardolph and Falstaff and the
play with the conscripts: Mouldy, whose old mother has no one else to
do "her husbandry and her drudgery"; the thin Shadow; the ragged
Wart; Feeble the woman's tailor, who has a stout heart and—like Hamlet—a philosophic mind;[8] Bullcalf who has a cough "caught with ring-
ing in the king's affairs upon his coronation-day"—all of them, though
two escape the press, "mortal men" who "owe God a death." Then the

[7] Dr. Tillyard (*Shakespeare's History Plays*, p. 303) aptly quotes Hardy's "In a
Time of the Breaking of Nations."
[8] "By my troth, I care not; a man can die but once; we owe God a death; I'll
ne'er bear a base mind: an't by my destiny, so; an't be not, so; no man's too good to
serve his prince; and let it go which way it will, he that dies this year is quit for
the next" (III.ii.230–4).

theme of times past—part memory, part make-believe—is taken up again. "Doth she hold her own well?" Shallow asks Falstaff of Jane Nightwork.

Falstaff. Old, old, Master Shallow.
Shallow. Nay, she must be old; she cannot choose but be old; certain she's old; and had Robin Nightwork by old Nightwork before I came to Clement's Inn.
Silence. That's fifty-five years ago.
Shallow. Ha, cousin Silence, that thou hadst seen that that this knight and I have seen! Ha, Sir John, said I well?
Falstaff. We have heard the chimes at midnight, Master Shallow.
Shallow. That we have, that we have, that we have; in faith, Sir John, we have: our watch-word was "Hem boys!" Come, let's to dinner; come, let's to dinner: Jesus, the days that we have seen! Come, come.

                                                        (III.ii.200–215)

3

Now there are obvious ways in which the dominant mood of the play can be related to the mood of so many of the Sonnets; for here before us we

> perceive that men as plants increase,
> Cheered and check'd even by the self-same sky,
> Vaunt in their youthful sap, at height decrease,
> And wear their brave state out of memory.

2 Henry IV, like the Sonnets, is permeated by "the conceit of this inconstant stay," and for an understanding of the play itself, as for any attempt to understand the Shakespearean progress, it is necessary to see how the constant sense of time—of time as mere sequence, bringing change—shapes the matter before us. Yet to put the matter thus, necessary as it is, is to give a partial and one-sided impression. Unqualified, the account so far given falsifies the imaginative impact of a play that is more lively, more complex, and more far-reaching in its implications than I have so far been able to suggest.

The tone of the play is sombre; but it could not possibly be called pessimistic or depressed. Not only is there the vigour of mind with which the political theme is grasped and presented; there is, in the Falstaff scenes, a familiar comic verve together with an outgoing sympathy—even, at times, liking—for what is so firmly judged. It is important, here, to say neither more nor less than one means, and humour is of all literary qualities the most difficult to handle. Where, as in Shakespeare or Jonson or Molière, humour serves a serious, a

truly imaginative purpose, the commentator who tries to define the
purpose is likely to cut an odd figure in the eyes of those whose gusto
prefers to dwell exclusively on the fun. And indeed there is something
comic in a pedagogic or literary-critical handling of things that make
you laugh. In *King Henry IV, Part II*, there is nothing, to my taste,
so funny as the scene of the mock-kings in *Part I*; but there is the
superb incoherence of Mrs. Quickly, there is Pistol's constant re-
creation of the dramatic part in which he lives,[9] there is the exquisite
absence of positive presence in Silence; and Falstaff, though he can
sometimes go through the motions of wit without the reality (a failure
that seems, on Shakespeare's part, deliberate), can still sometimes
surprise us with the sheer agility of his self-defence. These things are
there, and we can only suppose that the mind that created them
enjoyed them. But in relation to our larger themes the significance
for us is this: we know that we are dealing with a free mind—one that
is neither driven by, nor bent on driving, an "idea"; the sombre preoccupations are not obsessions.

And Shakespeare shows a further characteristic of great genius: he
can feel for, can even invest with dignity, those representative human
types who, in the complex play of attitudes that constitute his dramatic
statement, are judged and found wanting. When Falstaff celebrates
with Doll Tearsheet, at the Boar's Head Tavern, his departure for the
wars (II.iv), there is nothing comic in the exhibition of senile lechery.
Yet the tipsy Doll can move us with, "Come, I'll be friends with thee,
Jack: thou art going to the wars; and whether I shall ever see thee
again or no, there is nobody cares." And at the end of the scene Mrs.
Quickly too has her moment, when sentimentality itself is transformed
simply by looking toward those human decencies and affections for
which—the realities being absent—it must do duty:

> Well, fare thee well: I have known thee these twenty nine years, come
> peascod time; but an honester and truer-hearted man,—well, fare thee
> well.

There is nothing facile in Shakespeare's charity; it is simply that
Shakespeare, like Chaucer, is not afraid of his spontaneous feelings,
and his feelings are not—so to speak—afraid of each other.

Here, then, is one way in which the insistent elegiac note is both
qualified and deepened. There is yet another. We have already
noticed the repeated references to Falstaff's age and diseases. But it
is not only Falstaff who is diseased. Northumberland is sick, or
"crafty-sick"; the King is dying; and the imagery of disease binds the
individuals to the general action.

[9] See Leslie Hotson's essay, "Ancient Pistol," in *Shakespeare's Sonnets Dated and
Other Essays.*

> Then you perceive the body of our kingdom
> How foul it is; what rank diseases grow,
> And with what danger, near the heart of it.
>   (III.i.38–40)

The King speaks here the same language as the Archbishop who opposes him:

> . . . we are all diseased,
> And with our surfeiting and wanton hours
> Have brought ourselves into a burning fever,
> And we must bleed for it.
>   (IV.i.54–7)

Now disease is not simply, like old age, an inevitable result of time. Disease, in this play as in others, is associated with disorder originating in the will. The land is sick because of an original act of usurpation, and because of the further self-seeking of those who helped Bolingbroke to the throne, and because people like Falstaff think that "the law of nature" [10] is different from and can override the law of justice.

In the light of this we can understand why the feelings associated with time in this play are not simply feelings of pathos ("And is old Double dead?"). As Mr. Traversi has remarked in an excellent essay,[11] "allied to the idea of Time in this play is the conception of overruling necessity. . . . *Necessity* is a fact generally accepted by all the political characters. . . . All are 'time's subjects.' " Now it is certainly true that we are very much aware of time's power; all the strivings of the characters are shadowed by it. But the word "time" (or "times"), so frequently appearing, more often than not means the present age, the present state of affairs; and it is with "the times" in this sense that, again and again, there is associated the compulsion or "necessity" invoked by both sides in the political quarrel:

> We see which way the stream of time doth run,
> And are enforced from our most quiet shore
> By the rough current of occasion.

> The time misorder'd doth, in common sense,
> Crowd us and crush us to this monstrous form,
> To hold our safety up.[12]

---

[10] "If the young dace be a bate for the old pike, I see no reason in the law of nature but I may snap at him [Shallow]" (III.ii.325–7).

[11] *Scrutiny*, XV, 2, Spring, 1948. This essay is incorporated in Mr. Traversi's *Shakespeare from Richard II to Henry V* (1957).

[12] IV.i.70–3 (Vaughan's "shore"—Folio, "there"—is adopted by Professor Dover Wilson in the New Cambridge edition), IV.ii.33–5. Both these passages are spoken

28

L. C. Knights

"Time's subjects," in short, are men compelled because they are followers of that policy, or self-interest, which works and can only work, "on leases of short-number'd hours." [13] And it is because they accept the times—the world's standards, the shifting pattern of warring interests—that they are ruled by Time, that it is impossible for them to see the temporal process as other than absolute: "Let time shape, and there an end."

I hope this does not seem like putting Shakespeare on the rack of a demand for a moral at any price. Shakespeare never explicitly points a moral; and it will be some years before he fully reveals in terms of the awakened imagination why those that follow their noses are led by their eyes, or what it really means to be the fool of time. For the moment we are only concerned with the direction that his developing insight is taking; and it seems to me that what is coming into consciousness is nothing less than an awareness of how men make the world that they inhabit, an understanding of the relation between what men are and the kind of perceptions that they have about the nature of things. It is this growing awareness, linking the overt social criticism with the more deep-lying and pervasive concern with time's power, that explains our sense of fundamental issues coming to expression. It explains why the tone of *2 Henry IV* is entirely different from the detached observation of the earlier plays. In Act I, scene i, Northumberland, finding physic in the poison of ill news, throws away his crutch and "sickly quoif."

> Now bind my brows with iron; and approach
> The ragged'st hour that time and spite dare bring
> To frown upon the enraged Northumberland!
> Let heaven kiss earth! now let not Nature's hand
> Keep the wild flood confined! let order die!
> And let this world no longer be a stage
> To feed contention in a lingering act;
> But let one spirit of the first-born Cain
> Reign in all bosoms, that, each heart being set
> On bloody courses, the rude scene may end,
> And darkness be the burier of the dead!

---

by the Archbishop of York. Bolingbroke's version of affairs is similar: he had no intention of taking the throne from Richard, "But that necessity so bow'd the state, That I and greatness were compell'd to kiss" (III.ii.73–4); and of the rebellion against himself, "Are these things then necessities? Then let us meet them like necessities" (III.i.92–3).

[13] [Love] fears not policy, that heretic,
Which works on leases of short-number'd hours . . .
(Sonnet CXXIV)

These lines, placed as they are at the climax of the first scene of the play, are intended to be taken with deadly seriousness: this is what is implied in Northumberland's "aptest way for safety and revenge." If the note of horror seems momentarily to go beyond the prevailing mood of the play (it is a note more appropriate to *Lear* or *Macbeth*,[14] it is not discordant with that mood which, even without this vision of anarchy, is sombre enough.

Henry IV, Part II is markedly a transitional play. It looks back to the Sonnets and the earlier history plays, and it looks forward to the great tragedies. In technique too we are beginning to find that more complete permeation of the material by the shaping imagination which distinguishes the plays that follow it from those that went before.[15] The words do not yet strike to unsuspected depths (it is significant that some of the most vividly realized scenes in the play are in prose); but in the manner of its working the play is nearer to *Macbeth* than to *Richard III*; the imagery is organic to the whole, and the verse and prose alike are beginning to promote that associative activity that I have tried to define as the distinguishing mark of great poetic drama. It is this imaginative wholeness that allows us to say that Shakespeare is now wholly *within* his material. As a result the play has that doubleness which, as T. S. Eliot says, is a characteristic of the greatest poetry,[16] and the more obvious qualities of action, satire, humour and pathos are informed and integrated by a serious vision of life subjected to time.

[14] There are the obvious parallels—*King Lear*, IV.ii.29–50, *Macbeth*, IV.i.50–60; also, of course, *Sir Thomas More*, II.iv and *Troilus and Cressida*, I.iii.108–24. Of the passage quoted in the text Professor Dover Wilson aptly asks, "What does not Pope's famous conclusion to *The Dunciad* owe to it?"

[15] See D. A. Traversi's essay already referred to.

[16] Introduction to G. Wilson Knight's, *The Wheel of Fire*, p. xiv.

The Unity of *2 Henry IV*[1]

by Clifford Leech

It should perhaps be made clear that this is not a contribution
to the debate on Shakespeare's original planning of the Prince Henry
plays. It has been argued by Dover Wilson in *The Fortunes of Falstaff*
and in his New Cambridge edition, and by E. M. W. Tillyard in
Shakespeare's History Plays, that the two parts of *Henry IV* constitute
one long play, envisaged at least in its main outlines from the very
beginning of Part I. M. A. Shaaber, on the other hand, has put a
case for regarding Part II as a sequel, outside Shakespeare's original
plan, brought into being through the remarkable success of Part I.[2]
Whichever of these views is correct, it is possible for Part II to have
its own characteristic mood and structure, its separate dramatic
impact, and my concern will be to demonstrate that this is indeed
the case. The only assumption I shall make, which I think will be
readily granted to me, is that Part II was written after Part I.

In writing the series of eight plays which give an outline of English
history from the reign of Richard II to the accession of Henry VII,
Shakespeare can hardly at the beginning have seen the scheme as a
whole. If he had, it would be odd to start with the troubles of Henry
VI. The mention of Prince Henry near the end of *Richard II* suggests it was then that Shakespeare began to think of plays in which he
would be the central figure, plays which would close the gap between
Bolingbroke's usurpation and the funeral of Henry V. But clearly
the plays in the sequence already written had been markedly different from one another in structure and atmosphere. This was
partly, of course, because Shakespeare's grasp of play-making and

---

"The Unity of 2 Henry IV*"* by *Clifford Leech. From* Shakespeare Survey 6 *(New
York and London: Cambridge University Press, 1953), pp. 16–24. Reprinted by permission of the author and publisher.*

[1] This article is based on a paper read at the Shakespeare Conference, Stratford-
upon-Avon, in August, 1951.

[2] "The Unity of Henry IV," *Joseph Quincy Adams Memorial Studies,* 1948, pp.
217–27. Since this article was written, H. Edward Cain has supported Shaaber's case
in "Further Light on the Relation of *1* and *2 Henry IV*," *Shakespeare Quarterly,*
III (January, 1952), 21–38.

dramatic language was rapidly becoming more secure, but partly too it was because the action of each play had demanded a specific handling. There are recognizable distinctions in material and manner between the three *Henry VI* plays, and when Shakespeare continued the story with *Richard III* he employed a new massiveness and formality of structure in his presentation of a strong man who abused his sovereign power in the wanton exercise of his own will: Richard of Gloucester, the Samson in the devil's cause who brought down the temple upon himself, demanded a play in which all his followers and adversaries were reduced almost to a choric function, until Henry of Richmond came, as a god from over sea, to confront him. The play of *Richard II*, because Shakespeare saw the King as a man too conceited for scruple, complacent in his royalty, and yet with an exquisite taste in suffering, had necessarily a quieter tone, a more human presentation of the usurper, an elegiac note because this play marked the beginning of England's trouble. So, later on, with *Henry V*, the glorious interlude which had its centre in Agincourt was to be punctuated only with marks of exclamation, those chorus-passages directed at keeping the mind alight: the only conflict was that of arms, and for once it is not the sickness of the commonwealth that we are asked to consider, but the success of a foreign campaign. In describing these plays, I have of course simplified their effects. There are quieter, elegiac moments even in the grim ritual of *Richard III*; national glory is for a little, when Gaunt dies, the theme of *Richard II*; and there are passages in *Henry V* which demonstrate that the strife and intrigue of the previous reign are by no means done. Yet there is a dominant tone in each drama. Similarly, each of the two parts of *Henry IV* makes its characteristic and distinct impression on us.

When Shakespeare began to write of the youth of Prince Henry, he had indeed a subject that called for lightness of heart. Here was a young man, having his fun, yet not compromising himself so far that he could not later shine in council and on the field of battle. The civil troubles of his usurping father could not be shirked, but at least these troubles were manageable and might even afford some apprenticeship for the growing Prince. Coleridge has described *Romeo and Juliet* as a play given unity of feeling by the youth and spring-time that permeate every character and moment: even its old men, he says, have "an eagerness, a hastiness, a precipitancy—the effect of spring." [3] That might almost be our judgement too of *1 Henry IV*. There is a graver note in the portraits of the King and old Northumberland, but the dominant feeling is young, excited, good-hearted.

---

[3] *Coleridge's Shakespearean Criticism* (ed. Raysor, 1930), II, 265.

The Prince must not forget his future, must not think exclusively in terms of personal glory, as Hotspur does, must not think only of the moment's pleasure, as Falstaff does: but he can and should value these things, while recognizing their subordination to the obligations and opportunities that will come to him with the golden round. When seeing Part I, we may prefer the company of either Hotspur or Falstaff to that of the Prince, but we are not out of sympathy with him, and esteem him when he shows respect for Hotspur and liking for Falstaff. At the end of Part I, he has overcome Hotspur in single combat, an incident not found in Holinshed: he has revealed himself as the good and honourable fighter needed for the play of Agincourt.

In arguing that Part II was an "unpremeditated addition," which need not concern us here, R. A. Law[4] has emphasized the morality characteristics of that Part, the placing of Prince Henry between the personified representations of order (in the Lord Chief Justice) and disorder (in Falstaff). This account of the play's structure has been elaborated by Tillyard, though of course he disagrees with Law on the play's origin. It does indeed now seem beyond question that the Prince, no longer on the field of battle, is exhibited as slowly abandoning his old associations with disorder and becoming ultimately at one with its opposite. Not that we have a "conversion," as in the old moralities, but rather a manifestation of a hitherto concealed adherence. This part of the play's substance becomes most noticeable towards its end, when Falstaff is ready to steal any man's horses because his "dear boy" is on the throne, and Doll and the Hostess are taken to prison for being concerned in a man's death. To demonstrate this second phase in Hal's apprenticeship is the overt intention of this Part, as we may say that the overt intention of *Macbeth* is to demonstrate the ills that come upon a man and his country when he murders his King and steals the crown. But just as we may think that there is a secondary intention to *Macbeth,* to hint at a protest against the very frame of things, so in this Second Part of *Henry IV* we may feel that the dramatist, in giving us the preparation for Agincourt, hints also at a state of dubiety concerning basic assumptions in the great historical scheme. He shows us the new King adhering to political order, yet makes us half-doubt whether that order is worth its price, whether in fact it is of the deepest importance to men. And with this element of doubt, the poet's awareness of mutability grows more intense.

Whether Part II was a new play or a continuation of one already begun, the battle of Shrewsbury had marked the end of a phase.

[4] "Structural Unity in the Two Parts of *Henry the Fourth,*" *Studies in Philology,* XXIV (1927), 223-42.

Shakespeare, returning to his subject, and to a more sober aspect
of that subject (for law has not the manifest attractiveness of chivalrous
encounter), was bound to approach his task with less light-hearted-
ness, with a cooler and more objective view. Just as Marlowe in
Tamburlaine appears to see his hero with less enthusiasm in Part II
than in Part I, recognizing his excess as such and not keeping him
immune from ridicule, so here Shakespeare weighs his characters more
carefully and questions even the accuracy of his balance.

This note in the play is, I think, struck in the Induction itself.
Clearly Shakespeare needed an introductory speech here, both to
remind his auditors of what had happened at Shrewsbury and to
make plain the irony of the false news brought to Northumberland
in the first scene of the play. But he is not content with a simple
Prologue. His speaker is a quasi-morality figure, and no pleasant one.
Rumour expresses scorn for the credulity of men, and even—though
irrelevantly—for their love of slander. The scorn is brought home
when Rumour calls the audience he addresses "my household." In
tone this Induction is similar to the Prologue to *Troilus and
Cressida*: there too the speaker was in a costume appropriate to the
mood of the play—"A Prologue arm'd . . . suited in like conditions
as our argument"—and there too the tone was not gentle.

In the play we at once meet Northumberland, who has not gained
much of our affection in either of the two earlier plays in which he
appeared. Here he is the first of a series of old and sick men that we
are to encounter. Falstaff and Justice Shallow, King Henry IV and
the Lord Chief Justice, are all burdened with their years, and the
only one in full command of his wits and his body is the character
given no personal name and conceived almost as a morality-present-
ment of the Justice which he executes. Dover Wilson has drawn our
attention to the way in which our attitude to Falstaff is made to
change in the course of this Second Part,[5] though in concentrating on
the figures of Prince Hal and the Knight he does not perhaps fully
relate this change to the new atmosphere in the drama as a whole.
When we first meet Falstaff in I.ii, his talk is at once of his diseases,
and he reverts to this at the end of the scene when, like Ancient
Pistol in *Henry V*, he asserts his readiness to "turn diseases to commodity." There is, of course, plenty of gaiety in this talk of disease,
as there is in the scene with Doll at the Boar's Head: we delight in
the comedy of it, but the frailty of ageing flesh is grotesque as well as
amusing. Before we see "Saturn and Venus in conjunction," we are
told by the Drawers of how Falstaff was once "anger'd . . . to the
heart" when the Prince jested rudely on his age. The comedy here
and in Gloucestershire has a sharper savour because we are never

---

[5] *The Fortunes of Falstaff* (1943), pp. 93–8.

allowed to forget the evidence of decay. Justice Shallow, wrapping his thin frame in a fanciful tapestry of wild youth, is comedy of the rarest sort, but "Jesu, the days that we have seen!" is a line with a barb in it for us all. And the King, in his different way, belongs with these men. When we first meet him in Act III, he is longing for the sleep denied him; he cannot rid himself of guilt, ever more and more pathetically he talks of the crusade he will never make; and when he is dying he asks to be carried to the chamber called Jerusalem, so that the prophecy may be fulfilled and he may derive consolation from submitting to what has been decreed.

Along with the Falstaff scenes and the scenes at court, we have other parts of this play where a rebellion is launched and destroyed. This enterprise is contrasted sharply with the rebellion in Part I. There is no Hotspur to give dash and gaiety to it. His father is once more "crafty-sick," and the leadership of the revolt is in the grave hands of the Archbishop of York. He is not presented as a man scheming for advancement but as one who gives a measure of sanctification to the rebels' cause. Yet when they come together for the planning of their campaign, their language is hesitant, cautious, argumentative, as if they would talk themselves out of a situation from which there is no escape. At the end of L.i there is little hope in Northumberland's voice as he bids

> Get posts and letters, and make friends with speed:
> Never so few, and never yet more need.

And Hastings's concluding cry in I.iii—"We are time's subjects, and time bids, be gone"—has a fatalistic ring. It is no surprise to us when Northumberland's defection is shown, and it seems appropriate that these rebels, so given to sober talk, should be vanquished by a verbal trick before a blow is exchanged. In Holinshed it is not Prince John of Lancaster but the Earl of Westmoreland who dupes the rebels:[6] Shakespeare uses Westmoreland as an ambassador of Prince John, but gives to the King's son all the doubtful credit of the action. The change can, I think, only be explained by the assumption that Shakespeare wanted to bring this line of conduct more closely home to the royal house. Because Prince John is the King's son and Hal's brother, the stain of the exploit falls partly on them. Perhaps some will claim that such conduct was justified in the cause of law and order, that an Elizabethan would simply admire the skill of it. Yet is it possible not to find irony in John's concluding speech in the scene of Gaultree Forest?

---

[6] *The Historie of England* (1587), III, 529-30.

> I promised you redress of these same grievances
> Whereof you did complain; which, by mine honour,
> I will perform with a most Christian care.
>
> (IV.ii.113–15)

In the mouth of the astute Prince John the word "Christian" has an effect gross and palpable. When he proceeds to claim "God, and not we, hath safely fought to-day," we seem to recognize blasphemy. If this is not plain enough, one can turn to the next scene, where Falstaff demands from Prince John recompense for taking Sir John Colevile prisoner: he will otherwise, he says, see to his own glorification in ballad and picture: if that does not come to pass, he tells Prince John to "believe not the word of the noble." A few lines before we have seen the value of a noble's word in Gaultree Forest, and there is therefore strong irony in Falstaff thus exhorting Prince John. Nor should we overlook Shakespeare's reminder that Prince John's adroit handling of the situation is but a momentary trick. Hastings has told him that, if this revolt is put down, others will rise against the House of Lancaster:

> And though we here fall down,
> We have supplies to second our attempt:
> If they miscarry, theirs shall second them;
> And so success of mischief shall be born,
> And heir from heir shall hold this quarrel up,
> Whiles England shall have generation.
>
> (IV.ii.44–9)

To that John replies:

> You are too shallow, Hastings, much too shallow,
> To sound the bottom of the after-times.

It is Hastings who is right: John is too vain to see the total situation.

I have said that Shakespeare's substitution of Prince John for Westmoreland in the Gaultree affair brings the taint of it nearer to the King and Hal. When the play ends, and the new King has banished his old followers, the stage is empty except for Prince John and the Lord Chief Justice. Before mentioning the talk of French wars, Prince John spares a moment to praise his brother: "I like this fair proceeding of the king's," he says. It is surely not enviable to be praised by such men as Prince John. It is like Flamineo in *The White Devil* praising Brachiano's hypocritical display of grief for Isabella's death. Praise like that is a burden for a man to carry. We need not dispute that it was necessary to banish Falstaff if England was to be for a

time secure and Agincourt won. But we are made to realize that there
is a heavy price to pay for political success. Indeed, we are reminded
of it in the succeeding play, when, during the battle itself, Fluellen
refers to the rejection of the fat knight whose name he has forgotten.
In Shakespearian drama there is often a condition of tension between the play's overt meaning and its deeper implications. The gaiety
of *Twelfth Night* is enriched by the thread of sadness that runs
through it, but we cannot say that the baiting of Malvolio is in easy
accord with the play's surface texture. In *Macbeth* the enfolding of
the tragic idea within a morality pattern leaves us with a feeling of
suspended judgement in which we resent Malcolm's concluding
reference to "this dead butcher, and his fiend-like queen." So in this
Second Part of *Henry IV* the deeper, more disturbing implications
impinge directly on the main action of the drama, and then, as in
Macbeth, the writer appears to strain for the re-establishment of the
original framework. We get this feeling in the harshness of the words
that Henry V uses to Falstaff, for we have come to wonder a little
whether there is ultimately much to choose between Falstaff and
Prince John, and indeed we greatly prefer Falstaff's company. And the
same feeling emerges, I think, in the often praised scene where Hal is
reconciled to his father. Justifying his taking of the crown when he
believed his father dead, he says:

> I spake unto this crown as having sense
> And thus upbraided it: "The care on thee depending,
> Hath fed upon the body of my father;
> Therefore, thou best of gold art worst of gold.
> Other, less fine in carat, is more precious,
> Preserving life in medicine potable:
> But thou, most fine, most honour'd, most renown'd,
> Hast eat thy bearer up." Thus, my most royal liege,
> Accusing it, I put it on my head,
> To try with it, as with an enemy
> That had before my face murder'd my father,
> The quarrel of a true inheritor.
>
> (IV.v.158–69)

The elaborateness of the imagery is notable: the burden of the crown
is a devouring monster, its gold is contrasted to *aurum potabile,* it is
a murderer with whom the dead man's son must wage a blood-feud.
In this scene and in the new King's rejection of Falstaff, the note of
sternness and sobriety is heavily, almost clumsily, pressed down, in
an attempt to silence the basic questions that so often in the play
demand to be put. And perhaps, when he had done, Shakespeare
realized that this close was altogether too ponderous for a play that

had taken us to the Boar's Head and into Gloucestershire, and altogether too assured for a play persistently though not obtrusively concerned with change and ineradicable frailty. So he gave us the dancer's epilogue, in tripping prose, with its casual half-promise that Falstaff would come again in the next play: the banishment was to be merely from the King, and not from us. Later he was to change his mind again, perhaps because he realized that Sir John was no longer a figure of delight: around him had grown a small forest of disturbing thoughts, which might well choke the brief glory of Agincourt. *Henry V* was not the climax of a series, but rather an interlude, a holiday-play, in which for a while disaster was kept remote. Its epilogue does make plain that by this time Shakespeare had come to see his eight-play sequence as a whole, and within that sequence the Agincourt play must be predominantly sun-lit. He had to avoid, not too much gaiety with Falstaff, but too little. It is all the more remarkable that the questioning mood of *2 Henry IV* does show itself here and there in the succeeding play—with the intrigues of Canterbury and Ely; the frank presentation of many unchivalrous details of the war, from Bardolph's stealing of a "pax" to the King's twice-given order that every man shall kill his prisoners; the repeated reminder that a war-maker must have a just cause. But these things on the whole are kept in their place, and an audience for *Henry V* is not much disturbed in its dream of glory. In *2 Henry IV,* on the other hand, an audience is rarely at its ease.

In Law's paper on *Henry IV,* to which I have already acknowledged a debt, the darker side of Part II is in no way brought out. But Law does draw attention to the comic echoing of serious things in the play: Henry IV's sick memories of his early life are immediately followed, he points out, by Justice Shallow's maunderings on his deeds in the same period; Davy's petition to Shallow that "a knave should have some countenance at his friend's request" reminds us of Prince Hal's vigorous intercession for Bardolph with the Lord Chief Justice. There are a number of other ironic echoes in the play. At the end of the Boar's Head scene, when "a dozen captains" come to summon Falstaff to court, the Knight rises to the occasion, putting his rest from him:

> Pay the musicians, sirrah. Farewell Hostess; farewell Doll. You see, my good wenches, how men of merit are sought after: the undeserver may sleep, when the man of action is called on.

> (II.iv.403–6)

It is immediately after this that Henry IV has his famous utterance on the sleeplessness of kings. We are the less inclined to contemplate the ills of greatness with awe, because Falstaff has taken them to

himself already. We have noted the way in which Falstaff's "believe
not the word of the noble" comes immediately after the scene in
Gaultree Forest, but in III.ii there is an echo at Falstaff's expense.
In Part I he has this exchange with the Prince when the battle of
Shrewsbury is about to begin:

> *Fal.* I would 'twere bed-time, Hal, and all well.
> *Prince* Why, thou owest God a death.
> *Fal.* 'Tis not due yet; I would be loath to pay him before his day.
>
> (V.i.125–9)

Then there follows the "catechism" on "Honour." In Part II the
despised Feeble has a moment of splendour when, unlike Bullcalf
and Mouldy, he does not attempt to escape from impressment:

> By my troth, I care not; a man can die but once: we owe God a death:
> I'll ne'er bear a base mind: an't be my destiny, so; an't be not, so: no
> man is too good to serve's prince: and let it go which way it will, he that
> dies this year is quit for the next.
>
> (III.ii.250–5)

There is of course an absurdity in these words of bravery poured from
so weak a vessel, yet they demand respect. Bardolph's reply, "Well
said; thou'rt a good fellow," cannot be wholly ironic, and the im-
pressiveness of the effect is only mitigated, not destroyed, when Feeble
comes out again with his "Faith, I'll bear no base mind." The interplay of feelings in this Second Part is so complex that our sympathy
resides securely nowhere. Falstaff can be used to direct our feelings,
as he does with Prince John, and often through the play we prefer his
gross and witty animality to the politic management of the Lancastrians. But just as the dramatist makes no attempt to disguise his age
and sickness or even a churlish arrogance in him, so here he is put
down by Feeble's curious, inverted echo of his own words in the
First Part. I am of course not suggesting that Shakespeare could
expect an audience to note the echo: for us, however, it seems to
indicate a trend of feeling in the writer's mind.

The remarkable degree of objectivity in the presentation of the
characters reminds us of certain later plays of Shakespeare, those that
we call the "dark comedies." It is not merely through our latter-day
squeamishness, I believe, that we are made uneasy by the presentation
of the Duke and Isabella in *Measure for Measure*; and in *Troilus and
Cressida* Shakespeare's own Prologue warns us that the expectation of
armed strife is "tickling skittish spirits, On one and other side."
And *2 Henry IV* is close to these plays also in the peculiarly acrid
flavour of certain generalized utterances. On his first appearance in
the play, the King sees the process of time in geological change and

in the pattern of a human life, and there is no comfort in the vision, only a desire to have done:

> O God! that one might read the book of fate,
> And see the revolution of the times
> Make mountains level, and the continent,
> Weary of solid firmness, melt itself
> Into the sea! and, other times, to see
> The beachy girdle of the ocean
> Too wide for Neptune's hips; how chances mock
> And changes fill the cup of alteration
> With divers liquors! O, if this were seen,
> The happiest youth, viewing his progress through,
> What perils past, what crosses to ensue,
> Would shut the book, and sit him down and die.
>
> (III.i.45–56)

And when he is himself dying and he believes that his son has greedily seized the crown in advance of his right, he speaks of the human greed for gold, a theme no Elizabethan could long avoid, and how each generation is impatient for possession:

> See, sons, what things you are!
> How quickly nature falls into revolt
> When gold becomes her object!
> For this the foolish over-careful fathers
> Have broke their sleep with thoughts, their brains with care,
> Their bones with industry;
> For this they have engrossed and piled up
> The canker'd heaps of strange-achieved gold;
> For this they have been thoughtful to invest
> Their sons with arts and martial exercises:
> When, like the bee, culling from every flower
> The virtuous sweets,
> Our thighs pack'd with wax, our mouths with honey,
> We bring it to the hive, and, like the bees,
> Are murdered for our pains. This bitter taste
> Yield his engrossments to the ending father.
>
> (IV.v.65–80)

This is not far from what the Duke has to say to the condemned Claudio in *Measure for Measure*. Though he wears a friar's habit, he gives no religious consolation, but bids him see the vanity of existence, the impossibility of any sure possession, the cold impatience of an heir:

Friend hast thou none;
For thine own bowels, which do call thee sire,
The mere effusion of thy proper loins,
Do curse the gout, serpigo, and the rheum,
For ending thee no sooner.

(III.i.28–32)

It seems probable that 2 *Henry IV* was written some three years before
Troilus, some six before *Measure for Measure,* yet here Shakespeare
anticipates that objectivity of manner, fused with a suggestion of
deep and personal concern, which is characteristic of these two later
plays. The sequence of the histories depends on the cardinal assumption that order in a commonwealth is a prime good: it is not altogether
surprising that, as his task came towards its conclusion, and with the
additional effort required in writing a second play on a young king's
apprenticeship, Shakespeare should have reached a condition of
dubiety, should have felt less secure in his assumptions. The "dark
comedies" come during the tragic period, and in their way give
evidence of a similar slackening of grasp. The basic assumption made
by the tragic writer is that a personal goodness, inexplicable and apparently futile, can nevertheless be realized. But, unless the writer
has the sense of a direct revelation, this assumption can be maintained
only by strong effort: in the "dark comedies" the mind is not kept
tragically taut.

So far from demonstrating "the unity of 2 *Henry IV,*" it may appear
that I have shown only a clash of feelings within the play, an overt
morality intention, a preoccupation with the effects of time, and a
latent scepticism. That I would acknowledge, while maintaining that
such a contradiction persists in all the major plays of the Elizabethan
and Jacobean years. The tragic figures of the time are of great stature,
compelling our awe, but we are not spared realization that they can be
petty and grotesque and villainous as well. They are made to seem
free agents in their choice of good or evil yet simultaneously we are
made certain, from the beginning of the play, that destruction will
be theirs. So, in the best comedy, the gay march from wooing to
wedding, from pretence to its merry discomfiture, is counterpointed
with a low murmur of regret. Elizabethan dramas are rich in implication because they have emotional, but not logical, coherence. We
travel two roads, or more, at once. We arrive at no destination. But,
home again once more, we feel that—if we could but speak effectively
of such things—we should have travellers' tales to tell.

But it has been apparent, I think, that 2 *Henry IV* differs from
Part I in its dominant tone. Of course, there are sharp incidental
things in the earlier play, but they do not weigh heavily on the

spectator's mind. Falstaff abuses the press in both Parts, but his activities in this direction are shown at closer quarters in Part II. And there is broad merriment in the later play but it is worked into a pattern where good humour is not the main theme. Towards the end of Part II there is, indeed, a strong measure of simplification. From the Prince's last interview with his father to the rejection of Falstaff, Shakespeare strives to make the morality-element all-pervading, until we have the curious spectacle of Henry V urging repentance on his old companions: banishment was, of course, required, but he is an odd preacher to men whom kingship did not call to the disciplined life. And, as we have seen, the prose epilogue pretends that, after all, merriment is the prime concern of this play and the one to come. But, until Henry IV's death-scene, the delicate balance between the two layers of meaning is skilfully maintained.

When one is interpreting a Shakespeare play, one is always in danger of being reminded that Shakespeare was an Elizabethan, that his assumptions and standards of judgement were therefore different from ours. Tillyard has commented thus on Prince Hal's treatment of Francis in Part I:

> The subhuman element in the population must have been considerable in Shakespeare's day; that it should be treated almost like beasts was taken for granted.[7]

But is not this to overlook the fact that Shakespeare can make us resent the ill-treatment of any human being, and respect the most insignificant of creatures, a Feeble or a servant of the Duke of Cornwall? In *Measure for Measure* he reminds us even that an insect shares with us the experience of death and corporal suffering. He was an Elizabethan certainly: he made assumptions about kingship and "degree" and incest and adultery that perhaps we may not make. But he was also a human being with a remarkable degree of sensitivity: it is indeed for that reason that he can move us so much. If he merely had skill in "putting over" characteristic Tudor ideas, we could leave him to the social and political historians. Because his reaction to suffering, his esteem for good faith, his love of human society, his sense of mutability and loss, his obscure notion of human grandeur, his ultimate uncertainty of value, are not basically different from ours—though more deeply felt and incomparably expressed—he belongs supremely to literature. We do him, I think, scant justice if we assume that he could write complacently of Prince John of Lancaster, and could have no doubts about Prince Hal.

[7] *Shakespeare's History Plays* (1944), p. 277.

The Trial of Carnival in *Part Two*

by C. L. Barber

In *Part One,* Falstaff reigns, within his sphere, as Carnival; *Part Two* is very largely taken up with his trial. To put Carnival on trial, run him out of town, and burn or bury him is in folk custom a way of limiting, by ritual, the attitudes and impulses set loose by ritual. Such a trial, though conducted with gay hoots and jeers, serves to swing the mind round to a new vantage, where it sees misrule no longer as a benign release for the individual, but as a source of destructive consequences for society.[1] This sort of reckoning is what *Part Two* brings to Falstaff.

But Falstaff proves extremely difficult to bring to book—more difficult than an ordinary summer king—because his burlesque and mockery are developed to a point where the mood of a moment crystallizes as a settled attitude of scepticism. As we have observed before, in a static, monolithic society, a Lord of Misrule can be put back in his place after the revel with relative ease. The festive burlesque of solemn sanctities does not seriously threaten social values in a monolithic culture, because the license depends utterly upon what it mocks: liberty is unable to envisage any alternative to the accepted order except the standing of it on its head. But Shakespeare's culture was not monolithic: though its moralists assumed a single order, scepticism was beginning to have ground to stand on and look about —especially in and around London. So a Lord of Misrule figure, brought up, so to speak, from the country to the city, or from the traditional past into the changing present, could become on the Bankside the mouthpiece not merely for the dependent holiday scepticism which is endemic in a traditional society, but also for a dangerously self-sufficient everyday scepticism. When such a figure is set in an environment of sober-blooded great men behaving as

---

[1] The ritual of Carnival in Italy and its relation to Italian comedy has recently been exhibited in Professor Paolo Toschi's *Le origini del teatro italiano* (Torino, 1955) with a fullness and clarity made possible by the rich popular Italian heritage.

opportunistically as he, the effect is to raise radical questions about social sanctities. At the end of *Part Two,* the expulsion of Falstaff is presented by the dramatist as getting rid of this threat; Shakespeare has recourse to a primitive procedure to meet a modern challenge. We shall find reason to question whether this use of ritual entirely succeeds.

But the main body of *Part Two,* what I am seeing as the trial, as against the expulsion, is wonderfully effective drama. The first step in trying Carnival, the first step in ceasing to be his subjects, would be to stop calling him "My Lord" and call him instead by his right name, Misrule. Now this is just the step which Falstaff himself takes for us at the outset of *Part Two;* when we first see him, he is setting himself up as an institution, congratulating himself on his powers *as* buffoon and wit. He glories in his role with what Dover Wilson has aptly called "comic hubris." [2] In the saturnalian scenes of *Part One,* we saw that it is impossible to say just who he is; but in *Part Two,* Falstaff sets himself up at the outset as Falstaff:

> I am not only witty in myself, but the cause that wit is in other men. . . .
>
> A pox of this gout! or, a gout of this pox! for one or the other plays the rogue with my great toe. 'Tis no matter if I do halt. I have the wars for my colour, and my pension shall seem the more reasonable. A good wit will make use of anything. I will turn diseases to commodity.
>
> (I.ii.11–12, 273–78)

In the early portion of *Part One* he never spoke in asides, but now he constantly confides his schemes and his sense of himself to the audience. We do not have to see through him, but watch instead from inside his façades as he imposes them on others. Instead of warm amplifications centered on himself, his talk now consists chiefly of bland impudence or dry, denigrating comments on the way of the world. Much of the comedy is an almost Jonsonian spectacle where we relish a witty knave gulling fools.

It is this self-conscious Falstaff, confident of setting up his holiday license on an everyday basis, who at once encounters, of all awkward people, the Lord Chief Justice. From there on, during the first two acts, he is constantly put in the position of answering for his way of life; in effect he is repeatedly called to trial and keeps eluding it only by a "more than impudent sauciness" (II.i.123) and the privilege of his official employment in the wars. Mistress Quickly's attempt to arrest him is wonderfully ineffectual; but he notably fails to thrust the Lord Chief Justice from a level consideration. Hal and Poins

[2] *The Fortunes of Falstaff* (New York, 1944), Ch. V, "Falstaff High on Fortune's Wheel," p. 94.

then disguise themselves, not this time for the sake of the in-
comprehensible lies that Falstaff will tell, but in order to try him,
to see him "bestow himself . . . in his true colours" (II.ii.186). So
during the first two acts we are again and again put in the position
of judging him, although we continue to laugh with him. A vantage
is thus established from which we watch him in action in Gloucestershire, where the Justice he has to deal with is so shallow that Falstaff's
progress is a triumph. The comedy is still delightful; Falstaff is still
the greatest of wits; but we are constantly shown fun that involves
fraud. Falstaff himself tells us about his game, with proud relish.
Towards the end of the play, Hal's reconciliation with his father and
then with the Lord Chief Justice reemphasizes the detached vantage
of judgment. So no leading remarks are necessary to assure our noting
and marking when we hear Falstaff shouting, "Let us take any man's
horses; the laws of England are at my commandment. Blessed are
they that have been my friends, and woe unto my lord chief justice!"
(V.iii.140–144). The next moment we watch Doll and the Hostess
being hauled off by Beadles because "the man is dead that you and
Pistol beat among you" (V.iv.18).

Many of the basic structures in this action no doubt were shaped
by morality-play encounters between Virtues and Vices,[3] encounters
which from my vantage here can be seen as cognate to the festive and
scapegoat pattern. The trial of Falstaff is so effective *as drama* because no one conducts it—it happens. Falstaff, being a dramatic
character, not a mummery, does not know when he has had his day.
And he does not even recognize the authority who will finally sentence
him: he mistakes Hal for a bastard son of the king's (II.iv.307). The
result of the trial is to make us see perfectly the necessity for the
rejection of Falstaff as a man, as a favorite for a king, as the leader of
an interest at court.

But I do not think that the dramatist is equally successful in
justifying the rejection of Falstaff as a mode of awareness. The
problem is not in justifying rejection morally but in making the
process cogent *dramatically,* as in *Part One* we reject magical majesty
or intransigent chivalry. The bad luck which in *Part Two* Falstaff
goes about collecting, by shaking the black yak's tail of his wit over
people's heads, is the impulse to assume that nothing is sacred. In a
play concerned with ruthless political maneuver, much of it conducted by impersonal state functionaries, Falstaff turns up as a
functionary too, with his own version of maneuver and impersonality:
"If the young dace be a bait for the old pike, I see no reason in the
law of nature but I may snap at him" (III.ii.356–359). Now this attitude is a most appropriate response to the behavior of the high

³ *Ibid.,* pp. 17–22.

factions beneath whose struggles Falstaff plies his retail trade. In the Gaultree parleys, Lord John rebukes the Archbishop for his use of the counterfeited zeal of gentlemanly friendship to trick the rebels into disbanding their forces. The difference between his behavior and Falstaff's is of course that Lancaster has reasons of state on his side, a sanction supported, if not by legitimacy, at least by the desperate need for social order. This is a real difference, but a bare and harsh one. After all, Falstaff's little commonwealth of man has its pragmatic needs too: as he explains blandly to the Justice, he needs great infamy, because "he that buckles him in my belt cannot live in less" (I.iii.159–160).

The trouble with trying to get rid of this attitude merely by getting rid of Falstaff is that the attitude is too pervasive in the whole society of the play, whether public or private. It is too obviously *not* just a saturnalian mood, the extravagance of a moment: it is presented instead as in grain, as the way of the world. Shakespeare might have let the play end with this attitude dominant, a harsh recognition that life is a nasty business where the big fishes eat the little fishes, with the single redeeming consideration that political order is better than anarchy, so that there is a pragmatic virtue in loyalty to the power of the state. But instead the dramatist undertakes, in the last part of the play, to expel this view of the world and to dramatize the creation of legitimacy and sanctified social power. Although the final scenes are fascinating, with all sorts of illuminations, it seems to me that at this level they partly fail.

We have seen that Shakespeare typically uses ritual patterns of behavior and thought precisely in the course of making clear, by tragic or comic irony, that rituals have no *magical* efficacy. The reason for his failure at the close of *Part Two* is that at this point he himself uses ritual, not ironically transformed into drama, but magically. To do this involves a restriction instead of an extension of awareness. An extension of control and awareness is consummated in the epiphany of Hal's majesty while he is standing over Hotspur and Falstaff at the end of *Part One*. But *Part Two* ends with drastic restriction of awareness which goes with the embracing of magical modes of thought, not humorously but sentimentally.

It is true that the latter half of *Part Two* very effectively builds up to its finale by recurrent expression of a laboring need to be rid of a growth or humor. King Henry talks of the body of his kingdom as foul with rank diseases (III.i.39), and recalls Richard's prophecy that "foul sin gathering head / Shall break into corruption" (III.i.76–77). There are a number of other images of expulsion, such as the striking case where the rebels speak of the need to "purge th' obstructions which begin to stop / Our very veins of life" (IV.i.65–66). Henry

himself is sick in the last half of the play, and there are repeated suggestions that his sickness is the consequence both of his sinful usurpation and of the struggle to defend it. Since his usurpation was almost
a public duty, and his defense of order clearly for England's sake as
well as his own advantage, he becomes in these last scenes almost a
sacrificial figure, a king who sins for the sake of society, suffers for
society in suffering for his sin, and carries his sin off into death. Hal
speaks of the crown having "fed upon the body of my father" (IV.v.
160). Henry, in his last long speech, summarizes this pattern in saying:

> God knows, my son,
> By what bypaths and indirect crook'd ways
> I met this crown; and I myself know well
> How troublesome it sat upon my head.
> To thee it shall descend with better quiet,
> Better opinion, better confirmation;
> For all the soil of the achievement goes
> With me into the earth.
>   (IV.v.184–191)

The same image of burying sin occurs in some curious lines with
which Hal reassures his brothers:

> My father is gone wild into his grave;
> For in his tomb lie my affections . . .
>   (V.ii.123–124)

This conceit not only suggests an expulsion of evil, but hints at the
patricidal motive which is referred to explicitly elsewhere in these
final scenes and is the complement of the father-son atonement.

Now this sacrificial imagery, where used by and about the old
king, is effectively dramatic, because it does not ask the audience to
abandon any part of the awareness of a human, social situation which
the play as a whole has expressed. But the case is altered when Hal
turns on "that father ruffian" Falstaff. The new king's whip-lash lines
stress Falstaff's age and glance at his death:

> I know thee not, old man. Fall to thy prayers.
> How ill white hairs become a fool and jester!
> I have long dreamt of such a kind of man,
> So surfeit-swell'd, so old, and so profane;
> But being awak'd, I do despise my dream.
> Make less thy body, hence, and more thy grace;
> Leave gormandising. Know the grave doth gape
> For thee thrice wider than for other men.
>   (V.v.51–58)

The priggish tone, to which so many have objected, can be explained
at one level as appropriate to the solemn occasion of a coronation.
But it goes with a drastic narrowing of awareness. There are of course
occasions in life when people close off parts of their minds—a coronation is a case in point: Shakespeare, it can be argued, is simply putting
such an occasion into his play. But even his genius could not get
around the fact that to block off awareness of irony is contradictory
to the very nature of drama, which has as one of its functions the
extension of such awareness. Hal's lines, redefining his holiday with
Falstaff as a dream, and then despising the dream, seek to invalidate
that holiday pole of life, instead of including it, as his lines on his old
acquaintance did at the end of *Part One.* (Elsewhere in Shakespeare, to
dismiss dreams categorically is foolhardy.) And those lines about the
thrice-wide grave: are they a threat or a joke? We cannot tell, because
the sort of consciousness that would confirm a joke is being damped
out: "Reply not to me with a fool-born jest" (V.v.59). If ironies about
Hal were expressed by the context, we could take the scene as the rep-
resentation of his becoming a prig. But there is simply a blur in the
tone, a blur which results, I think, from a retreat into magic by the
dramatist, as distinct from his characters. Magically, the line about
burying the belly is exactly the appropriate threat. It goes with the
other images of burying sin and wildness and conveys the idea that the
grave can swallow what Falstaff's belly stands for. To assume that one
can cope with a pervasive attitude of mind by dealing physically with
its most prominent symbol—what is this but magic-mongering? It is
the same sort of juggling which we get in Henry IV's sentimental lines
taking literally the name of the Jerusalem chamber in the palace:

> Laud be to God! Even there my life must end.
> It hath been prophesied to me many years,
> I should not die but in Jerusalem . . .
>
> (IV.v.236–38)

One can imagine making a mockery of Henry's pious ejaculation by
catcalling a version of his final lines at the close of *Richard II* (V.vi.
49–50):

> Is this that voyage to the Holy Land
> To wash the blood from off your guilty hand?

An inhibition of irony goes here with Henry's making the symbol do
for the thing, just as it does with Hal's expulsion of Falstaff. A return
to an official view of the sanctity of state is achieved by sentimental use
of magical relations.

We can now suggest a few tentative conclusions of a general sort
about the relation of comedy to ritual. It appears that comedy uses

ritual in the process of redefining ritual as the expression of particular
personalities in particular circumstances. The heritage of ritual gives
universality and depth. The persons of the drama make the customary
gestures developed in ritual observance, and, in doing so, they project
in a wholehearted way attitudes which are not normally articulated at
large. At the same time, the dramatization of such gestures involves
being aware of their relation to the whole of experience in a way which
is not necessary for the celebrants of a ritual proper. In the actual
observance of customary misrule, the control of the disruptive motives
which the festivity expresses is achieved by the group's recognition of
the place of the whole business within the larger rhythm of their continuing social life. No one need decide, therefore, whether the identi-
fications involved in the ceremony are magically valid or merely expressive. But in the drama, perspective and control depend on presenting, along with the ritual gestures, an expression of a social situation
out of which they grow. So the drama must control magic by re-under-
standing it as imagination: dramatic irony must constantly dog the
wish that the mock king be real, that the self be all the world or set all
the world at naught. When, through a failure of irony, the dramatist
presents ritual as magically valid, the result is sentimental, since drama
lacks the kind of control which in ritual comes from the auditors' being
participants. Sentimental "drama," that which succeeds in being neither comedy nor tragedy, can be regarded from this vantage as theater
used as a substitute for ritual, without the commitment to participation
and discipline proper to ritual nor the commitment to the fullest
understanding proper to comedy or tragedy.

Historically, Shakespeare's drama can be seen as part of the process
by which our culture has moved from absolutist modes of thought
towards a historical and psychological view of man. But though the
Renaissance moment made the tension between a magical and an em-
pirical view of man particularly acute, this pull is of course always
present: it is the tension between the heart and the world. By incar-
nating ritual as plot and character, the dramatist finds an embodiment
for the heart's drastic gestures while recognizing how the world keeps
comically and tragically giving them the lie.

The Generations in 2 *Henry IV*

by *Robert B. Pierce*

2 *Henry IV* lacks the neat balance of characters and incident that in Part 1 develops the theme of Hal's growth toward readiness for kingship. Part 2 relies primarily on language and atmosphere to hold the sprawling set of historical and comic events together.[1] By these means Shakespeare focuses our attention on the theme of generations. Hal's relationship to the older generation defines the significance of his coronation, the climactic event of the play.

It is age rather than Hal's youth that dominates most of the play. 2 *Henry IV* is a play of old men fearfully and reluctantly letting go their grasp of power. As they lose control, they lose their sense of purpose, or else they fear that their code of values will be abandoned by the new generation. It is not only Hal's father who fears the prospect of a degenerate king. All of England misjudges the strength and integrity with which Hal will reign, because his intentions, and his relation to the traditions of the past, are concealed by a moral disguise.

Shakespeare's picture of a dying generation and the growth of a new one to succeed it is the most panoramic expression of his concern in the history plays with fathers and sons, with the inheritance of title, place, and moral code. The initial dramatic impression is one of age and decay.[2] First we see the aged Northumberland's crafty-sickness and then Falstaff's even less elegant ailment (whether syphilis or gout). But the primary symbolic fact of the play is the king's illness, which a number of the characters discuss before Henry appears "in his night-

---

"The Generations in 2 Henry IV*" by *Robert B. Pierce*. An unpublished essay. Printed by permission of the author.*

[1] On the use of time for this purpose see Benjamin T. Spencer, "2 *Henry IV* and the Theme of Time," *University of Toronto Quarterly*, XIII (July, 1944), 394–399, and L. C. Knights, *Some Shakespearean Themes* (London, 1959), pp. 51–64. See pp. 13–29. It might seem odd to give Falstaff a subordinate place in such a discussion. Whether 2 *Henry IV* was an afterthought, whether Falstaff grew beyond all reasonable compass because of his popularity in Part 1, or whatever the reason, he dominates the theatrical interest of Part 2. But Falstaff has received much critical attention, and his bulk can obscure significant patterns in the play as a whole.

[2] Cf. Clifford Leech, "The Unity of 2 *Henry IV*," *Shakespeare Survey 6* (1953), p. 18. See pp. 30–41.

49

gown." [3] The land declines in sympathy with its sick and dying king until its omens foretell his death. [4] The declining vigor of most of the characters gives the play an air of impersonality, as though superhuman forces rather than personalities were controlling events. In such a world an abstraction like Vergil's *Fama* belongs, and she appears in the Induction as "Rumour painted full of tongues" (s.d. at 1). Rumor's imagery recalls the more vigorous world of *1 Henry IV* when she reports that the king

> Hath beaten down young Hotspur and his troops,
> Quenching the flame of bold rebellion
> Even with the rebels' blood.
>
> (25-27)

Contrasting with this bold violence in the past is the scene to come, set in a "worm-eaten hold of ragged stone" (Induction, 35) where an old man lies feigning sickness to avoid the battle in which his son, his hope of posterity, has been killed.

What other play of Shakespeare's is so full of old, sick men who fear or long for death? Yet there is another quality even in some of the old men themselves. After all, Falstaff is one of them, and his explanation for his aged appearance contains a truth behind the impudent fantasy: "My lord, I was born about three of the clock in the afternoon, with a white head, and something a round belly. For my voice, I have lost it with hallooing, and singing of anthems" (I.ii.186–189). He shows the external signs of age without its deficiencies. Justice Shallow is the epitome of old age with his often-repeated, mendacious recollections of youth, his folly just covered by a thin cunning, and his feeble pride in his land and wealth, yet even he is associated with those ancient pastoral symbols of regeneration and growth, farming and raising flocks. Though less obviously than in Part 1, English life preserves something of its normal state, the quality that allows it to regenerate itself while the court declines under the strain of opposing the forces of disorder.

Still, age and decay dominate the foreground, and they bring with them a terrifying loss of order. Northumberland's Machiavellianism has lost its coherency, thinned down to spasms of rage and despair.

---

[3] *The Second Part of King Henry IV*, ed. A. R. Humphreys, New Arden Shakespeare (Cambridge, Mass., 1966), s.d. at III.i.1. All quotations are taken from Humphreys' text.

[4] The close bond between king and kingdom, a commonplace of Renaissance political theory, is suggested by the habit of referring to a king by the name of his land—England, France, or whatever. Erasmus repeats a commonplace when he says, "What the heart is in the body of a living creature, that the prince is in the state." *The Education of a Christian Prince*, trans. Lester K. Born (New York, 1936), pp. 175–176.

Hearing of Hotspur's death, he starts to vow revenge, but drifts into a fascinated vision of chaos:

> Let heaven kiss earth! Now let not Nature's hand
> Keep the wild flood confin'd! Let order die!
> And let this world no longer be a stage
> To feed contention in a ling'ring act;
> But let one spirit of the first-born Cain
> Reign in all bosoms, that, each heart being set
> On bloody courses, the rude scene may end,
> And darkness be the burier of the dead!
>
> (I.i.153–160)

Affirming disorder is a self-destructive act, and Northumberland's passion ebbs into a decision once again to betray his fellow conspirators and take refuge in flight. His weakness is only the most striking example of how the great Percy rebellion tapers off into squabbling and overreached policy. For all its fine dark splendor in Part 1, rebellion dies of age and internal rot in this play.

Henry IV is wiser and nobler than his opponents. At least he believes in order and shows a real concern for his kingdom's welfare. Yet he too is a sick old man trapped between policy and ideal. He wants to affirm the great principle of royal inheritance. With the crown he wants to pass on to his son the kingdom's loyalty and the royal tradition of heroic rule, all embodied in the past glories of Edward III. Because he has stolen the crown, however, he is punished by disorder. He cannot trust the loyalty of his own supporters, who rise against him, and Hal's wildness seems another punishment for his usurpation. The man who has broken the chain of inheritance finds no trace of moral inheritance in his son. Symbolic of his dilemma is his projected crusade: it springs from a desperate hope for expiation, for escape from guilt and civil war to an unambiguous war of pious glory. But we learn in his interview with Hal that policy has tainted this plan, since the crusade is to distract the nobles, whom he still dares not trust. Even this equivocal purgation is denied him. All the court know that his illness makes the crusade impossible, and by a grotesque pun he dies in the Jerusalem Chamber, not the holy city of Jerusalem.

Even while throwing off rebellion, the king and his kingdom visibly decline. Though order is maintained, it becomes more and more an empty pattern. The rebels have nothing better to offer than the court, only chaos or that dreadful anti-pattern of inherited hatred that Hastings predicts:

> And though we here fall down,
> We have supplies to second our attempt:
> If they miscarry, theirs shall second them;

And so success of mischief shall be born,
And heir from heir shall hold this quarrel up
Whiles England shall have generation.

(IV.ii.44–49)

For all of Henry's victories, the monstrous order of disorder which dominates the Henry VI plays seems near. Henry does represent a kind of order in the land, and it is through his blood and the virtues he stands for that Hal is tied to the great royal tradition. Henry IV sums up both the declining England that must be regenerated and the past values out of which such regeneration must spring.

The central critical problem of the play is to decide Hal's relation to this dilemma. Does he inherit only his father's Machiavellian policy, screened by a hypocritical piety?[5] Does he regenerate England even while retaining an ambiguous morality, one perhaps inherent in political rule?[6] Or does he combine the virtues of the past with a youthful renewal of spirit, leading England into a heroic age?[7] The choice among these possibilities depends on Shakespeare's handling of two romance motifs, the legend of Hal the wild prince and the theme of royalty in disguise.

Though the wastrel reformed is an old and widespread motif, Shakespeare's historical sources directly offer the legend of a reckless young prince who abruptly and completely reforms at his father's death. *The Famous Victories of Henry the Fifth* shows this conversion at its most arbitrary,[8] and Shakespeare keeps part of the romance unreality from his material. In particular the twin conversions of Part 1 and Part 2 are not completely harmonized, though even in that the trend is toward naturalistic drama.[9] The dramatic problem is how to turn a disreputable young prince suddenly into a hero-king.

[5] For one modern follower of Hazlitt's antipathy to Hal, see Harold C. Goddard, *The Meaning of Shakespeare* (Chicago, 1951), pp. 161–214.

[6] There is a thorough and forceful statement of this view in Derek Traversi, *Shakespeare from Richard II to Henry V* (London, 1958), pp. 108–165.

[7] Classical statements of this view are in John Dover Wilson, *The Fortunes of Falstaff* (Cambridge, 1943), and E. M. W. Tillyard, *Shakespeare's History Plays* (London, 1944), pp. 264–304.

[8] Hal is shown as a thorough scoundrel, a highwayman. He wishes for his father's death and comes to his sickbed with a dagger in his hand. The king's tears and reproaches yield a sudden and complete reformation, though there is later the misunderstanding over the crown. Geoffrey Bullough discusses the connection of the two plays in *Narrative and Dramatic Sources of Shakespeare*, IV (New York, 1962), 256–262. William Glasgow Bowling, "The Wild Prince Hal in Legend and Literature," *Washington University Studies*, XIII (April, 1926), 305–334, argues that the legend includes a residuum of historical fact. At any rate, by Shakespeare's time the facts had been assimilated to a romance pattern.

[9] Hal is plausible enough, as I shall suggest below. The inconsistency is in the other characters' apparent forgetfulness of his reform in *1 Henry IV*.

In *1 Henry IV* Shakespeare patterns Hal on the Prodigal Son figure frequent in Renaissance ethical drama, but in Part 2 his solution is somewhat different. The Prodigal Son form is minimized, and Hal assimilates and develops another pattern, that of the king or prince in disguise.[10] This motif is common in Elizabethan drama, as in the two popular plays *George à Greene* and *Friar Bacon and Friar Bungay*.[11] Its appeal is clear: it suggests the essential oneness of king and people since in disguise he can associate with them as equals. Even the monarch is after all a "king of good fellows," as Henry V calls himself before Katherine, whom he woos in good country style. Yet implicit in disguise is the other side. Only when he is unrecognized, only as Harry LeRoy, can the king be just a good fellow among the people. In his own name he is the king, sacred, untouchable, and lonely, with all the pathos that Shakespeare gives to that loneliness. Henry V can quarrel with Michael Williams as an equal, yet that same quarrel kindles a soliloquy on the king's heavy isolation.

At one point in *2 Henry IV* Hal actually puts on a disguise when he and Poins transform themselves into drawers in order to spy on Falstaff. Hal comments sardonically on the effect: "From a god to a bull? A heavy descension! It was Jove's case. From a prince to a prentice? A low transformation! that shall be mine, for in everything the purpose must weigh with the folly." [12] (II.ii.166–169) Hal's disguise allows him to hear Falstaff picturing him in ordinary terms indeed, but the knight's description is typically unrelated to reality, as he admits when Hal reveals himself. The physical disguise stands for no inner degradation, though it represents the whole land's opinion of Hal.

Hal's self-concealment in the play is not, however, primarily physical. Shakespeare solves his dramatic problem by giving him a moral disguise, so that all around him misjudge his nature. Hal is consistently ironic, aware of the discrepancy between what he seems and what he will prove to be. He can descend to be a drawer because the genuine Hal stands back and comments. The ingenuity of this device is that it leaves ambiguous just what the real Hal is and so makes the conversion

[10] John Lawlor refers allusively to this element in Chapter 1, "Appearance and Reality," of *The Tragic Sense in Shakespeare* (London, 1960), pp. 17–44.

[11] These plays illustrate the two potentialities of the motif. In *George à Greene* King Edward proves himself a man of his people, in particular when he vails his staff to the shoemakers of Bradford. The emphasis is on kingly humanity. Prince Edward of *Friar Bacon and Friar Bungay*, though attracted to fair Margaret, the low-born natural aristocrat, overcomes his passion with the magnanimity of royal blood.

[12] I do not believe the pun on "case" has been commented upon. It means both "state" and "costume or outer garb." At the risk of pushing a metaphor too hard, I would suggest that the second sense implies a common truth: neither Jove, lord of the skies, nor Hal, the future king, destroys his essential being by disguise. Both are "essentially made without seeming so." (*1HIV*, II.iv.486–487)

more plausible. Warwick portrays Hal as wholly untainted, if rather calculating for modern tastes:

> The Prince but studies his companions
> Like a strange tongue, wherein, to gain the language,
> 'Tis needful that the most immodest word
> Be look'd upon and learnt; which once attain'd,
> Your Highness knows, comes to no further use
> But to be known and hated.
>
> (IV.iv.68–73)

The implication of this speech is that there can be no real bond between a king and lower men, that he must know them only to reject them.[18] Yet Warwick seems to be reassuring the old king in the face of his own less sanguine view. He is as gloomy as the rest when Hal succeeds to the throne (V.ii.14–18). If Hal's disguise is just policy, he has deceived everyone.

Surely, however, the truth is more complex. Shakespeare uses disguise ambiguously in his plays: it both conceals and manifests identity. Rosalind and Viola hide their femininity in boys' clothes, yet both can express themselves the more fully for their disguise. In donning a friar's robes and acting as spiritual guide, the Duke in *Measure for Measure* adopts the sacred equivalent of his secular position, and the two roles enrich each other. In the same way Hal manifests himself in disguise, even frees a part of his nature that the court stifles. Not only does he escape the formality of the court and develop the oneness with his kingdom that is the basis of true royalty, but he gets beyond the guilt of his tainted inheritance by renewed contact with the people, the source of royal power.

When Hal enters the play, he appears subdued to the overall tone of gloom and decline: "Before God, I am exceeding weary" (II.ii.1). He has just returned from fighting the rebels, and he reveals shortly that he is grieving at his father's illness. Shrewsbury seems to have solved nothing. He is terribly conscious of his ordinary humanity, the obverse of his royal position. He can laugh at this side of himself and almost regains his spirits in the course of his witty description of Poins's linen, but Poins's inadequacy as a companion makes itself obvious at this moment. He uses Henry IV's illness as a weapon in the battle of wits, oblivious to the sincerity of Hal's grief. Hal is driven further into his characteristic irony by this jesting, and the irony now has a tone of self-contempt that embitters his wit.

[18] Again Erasmus is typical of Renaissance moralists: "The common run of princes zealously avoid the dress and manner of living of the lower classes. Just so should the true prince be removed from the sullied opinions and desires of the common folk." Erasmus, p. 150.

Hal tells Poins that he is seeking London life rather than attending his father because he does not want to seem like a hypocrite. Although his words show that he is not really insensitive to his father, he is again rationalizing his wildness, as in the soliloquy in *1 Henry IV*, I.ii. In fact he is fleeing from his grief into dissipation, and the result is that a companion like Poins necessarily misunderstands him. Because Hal is conscious of his irresponsibility, his irony remains strongly in force. Still his spirits pick up in the wit play, and by the end of the scene he is launched on the boyish prank of spying on Falstaff. His gloom penetrates no deeper than his apparent corruption.

Poised against Hal's energetic prose in this and the scene with Falstaff is the solemn blank verse with which Henry IV enters the play in III.i, brooding on the woes of kingship and the vagaries of fate. With genuine nobility he turns to a fatalistic resolution, the only responsible moral position in a determined world such as that which Warwick portrays and he accepts. The two styles of Hal and Henry and the men implied in them might seem irreconcilable, yet ironically enough a further misunderstanding, Hal's taking away the crown, brings them together.

Hal enters in IV.v full of spirits, partly from the good war news, but his mood is sobered by his father's relapse. As he sits by his father's bed (an "office of love," as R. P. Cowl points out[14]), he addresses the crown in a blank-verse soliloquy full of the feeling of Henry's apostrophe to sleep. His words balance filial sorrow and consciousness of inheritance:

> Thy due from me
> Is tears and heavy sorrows of the blood,
> Which nature, love, and filial tenderness
> Shall, O dear father, pay thee plenteously.
> My due from thee is this imperial crown,
> Which, as immediate from thy place and blood,
> Derives itself to me.
>
> (IV.v.36–42)

His grief is "of the blood," both deeply felt and natural, moved by the bond of kinship. At the same time he takes on with proper dignity the "lineal honour" (45) of his new royalty. Like his father he is concerned with the pattern of succession that will in time give his son the same crown. The Hal of 2 *Henry IV* can bridge the enormous gulf between Falstaff and Henry in both his emotions and his language. He can accept both energy and order.

14 *The Second Part of King Henry the Fourth*, ed. R. P. Cowl (London, 1923), n. at IV.v.19.

Misled by Hal's moral disguise, Henry forecasts a terrifying collapse
of order, destroying his aims and his kingdom. Again as in Part 1 Hal
must justify himself to his father. The tact and dignity with which
he does so are convincing proof of his moral readiness for his approaching duties. He can allude only briefly to his purposed reformation as king, since his father charges him with anticipating that
time too eagerly. But the real source of Henry's pain is Hal's apparent
lack of filial love. In reply Hal uses the language of commitment to
the order of the family. He makes his kneeling for pardon a symbol of
"my most inward true and duteous spirit" (147) and even his taking
the crown "The quarrel of a true inheritor" (168) against its cruelty.
In the latter explanation he can tell only half the truth (contrast his
words at 40–46 with his report of them in 158–164), because a father
hungering for love does not want to be told of his son's self-confident
readiness to replace him in the orderly succession of royalty. He strikes
exactly the right note in showing his sense of the cares that go with the
crown. His words proclaim sympathy for his father while proving that
he is not too ambitious. That is not to say that he plays hypocritically
on Henry's emotions. The genuineness of his love is shown both by his
tears and by his dignified but pointed references to his own grief.

The passionate relief of Henry's reply shows how successful Hal's
defense of taking the crown has been. He sees the judgment of Hal's
reply as well as its affection, and so he opens his political stratagems
more plainly than ever before. For the first time his less than peniten-
tial motive for the crusade emerges, and he counsels Hal to follow this
plan by stimulating "foreign quarrels" (214). His guilt has immersed
him in the disorder that ever yields new disorder, though his understanding of the dilemma shows that in some degree he has transcended
the guilt. Whereas he seized the throne, Hal is successive heir, but that
can be so only because Henry is indeed king. Hal can claim the throne
unequivocally, as his father could never do. In that strength he sur-
passes his father.

As in *1 Henry IV*, the private reconciliation leads to a public expression of Hal's worth. In Part 1 he demonstrates chivalric merit at
Shrewsbury, and in Part 2 he gives public assent to justice, the final
measure of a king.[15] When the Lord Chief Justice discusses the old
king's death with Henry's younger sons and Warwick, they all look
forward with dread to Henry V's reign. He enters and senses their fear,
which he sets out with fine tact to allay. He treats his brothers as fellows in a family, but also as representatives of a royal heritage. Now
he is both their king and head of their family:

---

[15] Both Wilson and Tillyard discuss this theme. Wilson sums up on p. 17, Tillyard
on pp. 264–266.

> For me, by heaven, I bid you be assur'd,
> I'll be your father and your brother too;
> Let me but bear your love, I'll bear your cares.
>
> (V.ii.56–58)

Thus order has passed from the old generation to the new; Hal is both his father reborn and something more.

When he turns to the Lord Chief Justice, a bit of his ironic disguise returns, albeit subdued to his new dignity. He allows the old man to think that he is still angry at having been imprisoned and so draws forth an impassioned defense of the rule of justice over all men, even a prince:

> Be now the father, and propose a son,
> Hear your own dignity so much profan'd,
> See your most dreadful laws so loosely slighted,
> Behold yourself so by a son disdain'd:
> And then imagine me taking your part,
> And in your power soft silencing your son.
>
> (V.ii.92–97)

By giving Hal a significant imaginary role, the Chief Justice teaches that one cannot violate the laws of the state without attacking the whole moral order, even the bonds of family. All the more must a prince submit to the laws of the king his father. Hence his severe justice has defended fatherhood as well as order in the state. Hal accepts this truth for himself and his posterity. Declaring to the Chief Justice, "You shall be as a father to my youth," (118) he takes up the total responsibility of his calling. Hal has become Henry V, which is to say that he is a king, but also that he is a man assuming his moral inheritance. He must cast off his disguise and the escape it temporarily affords so that he can affirm his bond with the noblest of the past. If he must reject Falstaff and the irresponsible pleasures of his youth to do so, he takes that step firmly as he turns to the emblem of kingly justice.

Falstaff, the Prince, and the History Play

by Harold E. Toliver

A rational eighteenth-century man of letters such as Maurice Morgann would undoubtedly bristle a little at our abandon in destroying his premises. He would have difficulty recognizing our portraits of Henry IV, for example, whom, in his simplicity, he had thought to be a rather impressive king despite a certain weakness at first for another man's crown. And he would be even more mystified by Henry V as Machiavellian strongman and confused war-maker. Ignorant of Frazer and Freud, he would not think to look for the key to the complexity and interest of Falstaff, the "whoreson, obscene, greasy tallow-catch," in ritualistic and magical analogues;[1] he would probably want to ask whether critics ought to be getting into such things in the first place, and if so, how the a-rational elements of motivation, imagery, and symbolic action, if they exist, can be made intelligible. For when we consider these elements, the discussion of "character" in the sense of certain definite traits appears extremely limited, and concepts of form naturally grow more uncertain as response to character shifts. Hence, the question of what *kind* the history play belongs to can no longer be answered in strictly Aristotelian terms.[2] Once over the initial shock,

---

[1] See C. L. Barber's essay, "Saturnalia in the Henriad," which is printed in *Shakespeare: Modern Essays in Criticism*, ed. Leonard F. Dean (New York, 1957), pp. 169–191, and in *Shakespeare's Festive Comedy*. Cf. J. I. M. Stewart, *Character and Motive in Shakespeare* (Bristol, 1949), p. 127; Northrop Frye, "The Argument of Comedy," *English Institute Essays* (149), p. 71; and Philip Williams, "The Birth and Death of Falstaff Reconsidered," SQ, VIII (1957), 359–365.

[2] The most complete attempts to arrive at a working concept of the history play *sui generis* are Irving Ribner's "The Tudor History Play: An Essay in Definition," PMLA, LXIX (1954), 591–609 and *The English History Play in the Age of Shakespeare* (Princeton University Press, 1957), pp. 1–32; H. B. Charlton's *Shakespeare: Politics and Politicians*, The English Association Pamphlet no. 72 (1929), pp. 7, 11, 13; Una Ellis-Fermor, *The Frontiers of Drama* (London, 1945), pp. 5–14, 34–55; Felix Schelling, *The English Chronicle Play* (New York, 1902); G. K. Hunter, "Shakespeare's Politics and the Rejection of Falstaff," *Critical Quarterly*, I (1959), 229–236. See also Coleridge's *Literary Remains*, H. N. Coleridge, ed. (London, 1836),

however, the traditional rationalist might discover certain fruitful interactions between his approach to the history play and modern approaches. In the matter of the relative place of comic and heroic figures in the history play, for example, the neoclassicist's sense of "decorum" —of a form following certain laws of plot, character, and language— might be made to engage more profoundly the raw stuff of the human psyche and its institutions and rituals imitated in the form. And in return, we might have to admit that while it may not be necessary for all purposes to read history plays under the auspices of a category, we gain from being aware that they are not simply studies in isolated problems of motivation, or fragments of primitive ritual. They do indeed have "form," as some kings have "character." Approaching the history play through either perspective by itself is likely to leave us unsatisfied, as though we had gone hunting kudu and flushed jerboa.

For the history play at its best attempts to do more than evoke purely chauvinistic emotion through heroic pageantry and spectacle, as it was once assumed; and it is not totally incapable of containing its Saturnalian kings of misrule and its Oedipal overtones in a form that transcends and orders them. Shakespeare, at least, appears to have sought in the history play a fresh artistic form capable of integrating providential order, pragmatic political concerns, and timeless human impulses.[3] One of the primary effects of that integration is an adjustment between inner and outer worlds, both in the hero and, since the history play is more nationalistic and "rhetorical" than other dramatic forms, through the hero in the audience, didactically. In ethical matters, the

VI, 16off.; A. C. Bradley, *Oxford Lectures on Poetry* (London, 1909), pp. 247–275; John Palmer, *Political Characters of Shakespeare* (London, 1945), pp. 184ff.; W. H. Auden, "The Fallen City: Some Reflections on Shakespeare's *Henry IV*," *Encounter*, XIII, no. 5 (1959), 25; and of course, Maurice Morgann, *An Essay on the Dramatic Character of Sir John Falstaff*, first published in 1777. Northrop Frye's *Anatomy of Criticism* is stimulating as usual, especially the following remarks: "The History merges so gradually into tragedy that we often cannot be sure when communion has turned into catharsis," and "The central theme of Elizabethan history is the unifying of the nation and the binding of the audience into the myth as the inheritors of that unity, set over against the disasters of civil war and weak leadership" (pp. 283–284). Finally, A. P. Rossiter's brief book *English Drama from Early Times to the Elizabethans* (London, 1950) illuminates the "mungrell" forms brilliantly.

I have not attempted here to comment on the structural problems raised by the linking of plays not only separate but inconsistent in many respects. Nothing essential to my concerns demands more than a minimum of demonstrable continuity in the series.

[3] Shakespeare's experimentation with the form is clear from the varieties he tried and from devices such as Rumour's induction to *2 Henry IV* (which suggests the uncertainty of historical events as experienced and yet offers the broader vision of the chronicler who sees everything with accuracy) and the chorus in *Henry V*, which moves the play toward dramatized epic.

adjustment is between the inner conscience and the amoral demands of political life; in economic motives, between personal and collective "property"; and in broadly social and religious matters, between the old Adam who takes his fixed place in the ranks or at Whitehall.

These adjustments involve the audience in a communal "rhythm" through a language generally more openly incantational than the language of Shakespearian tragedy and ritualistic in a different sense. For more than one kind of ritual and one kind of magic is involved in dramatic action. In a broad sense, "ritual" means any closely patterned visual ceremony or rhythmic language that engages the emotions of its participants and fuses them into a harmonious community. Both spectacle and rhythm work by raising like emotions throughout an audience and providing a common symbolic or "pulsing" medium for their transmission. Some rituals depend upon primitive forms of magic, and Falstaff, as J. I. M. Stewart, C. L. Barber, and Philip Williams believe, reflects certain fragments of them. But others become assimilated into sophisticated art and are consciously manipulated as one of its dimensions. In less primitive forms, they work not only through contact with highly charged currents from the subconscious, which criticism, as Morgann conceived of it, is ill-equipped to deal with, but also through a complex assortment of powers released by formal art. In the rejection scene, for example, the ritual of the new king depends upon the total of thematic, imagistic, and formal pressures brought to bear by the whole play or series of plays—and their social and political context. If tragic ritual reconciles the audience to a higher destiny of some sort, perhaps to the power of the gods or to a world of suffering beyond the protagonist's control, the ritual of the history play aims somewhat lower, at adjustment to political life—which may be thought to reveal destiny also, but destiny at least *filtered through* a social medium.

Social and political context is thus especially important in the history play, which in England developed under special historical conditions that caused it to rise and decline rapidly as literary types go. Though other dramatists experimented with it, Shakespeare (with the possible exception of the anonymous author of *Woodstock*) was the only one to see its full potential as a separate form. In his variation, it appealed strongly to an audience prepared to see it in a certain way, or in Mr. Barber's term, to "participate" in its special kind of ritualized nationalistic emotion. Like English tragedy, it arose partly out of the old morality and mystery plays; but onto these it grafted chronicle accounts of past events, folk-lore, native myth, and a new spirit of nationalism, all of which it shaped into moral patterns designed to bring out the providential guidance, the "meaning," of history. Since an audience removed from the original context cannot "participate" in historical ritual with the same intensity as an Elizabethan royalist who believed in the king's divine prerogatives, the historical context and content create problems that are less obtrusive in other dramatic forms, if present at all. But despite its inherent shortcomings, the history play at its best (in the series of plays from *Richard II* to *Henry V*) achieves an essentially new structure and dramatic rhythm, both peculiar to itself and effective.

Some aspects of that structure are borrowed from comedy and tragedy, and here again the neoclassicist, if put to the test, might be quick to see some aspects of the blend that others would overlook. Aristotle's concept of *anagnorisis* and *catharsis* would seem relevant, for example, in describing Falstaff's role as tragic victim—only one role among several, needless to say, but involved and crucial.[4] In one aspect the "plot" of *2 Henry IV* can be taken as a *mixed variation* of comic and tragic action, culminating in a sacrificial act with the new king acting as personal vicegerent for destiny. The effectiveness of the rejection speech as incantation depends upon our seeing the accumulated evidence as to the way of a world that Falstaff has affronted and does not fit, a world *requiring* a certain political order that cannot tolerate Falstaff as Chief Justice. The evidences of tragic form are clear enough before that, once we set aside the oversimplified notion that a figure must be either comic or tragic and not both. The implications of Falstaff's childlike self-love and hedonism from the beginning of *1 Henry IV* compose, in Francis Fergusson's Jamesian analogy, one of a set of "mirrors" reflecting the central action, the search for an effective adjustment between the inner self and the collective social organism. Since the aim of this action is ultimately to "redeem time" (and thus to redeem the times),[5] both in the sense of justifying "history" and in reconciling the audience to its historical role, Falstaff is best seen as a rebel against history, as guilty of *hubris* as he is of Saturnalian misrule.

The Falstaffian mirror, of course, is not entirely separable from the others. In Part One, the opening scenes reflect various inner-outer disturbances for which partial and ineffective cures are proposed. Bolingbroke's opening speech, for example, suggests a relatively easy, pragmatic cure for the illness of the state, which he describes in his own terms, a cure demanding only that the right people get the point quickly enough:

[4] This role has been mentioned occasionally but has not been extensively explored. See D. A. Traversi, *An Approach to Shakespeare* (New York, 1956), p. 32, and *Shakespeare from Richard II to Henry V* (Stanford University Press, 1957), pp. 77ff.; Stewart, pp. 127ff.; Auden, p. 25; Williams, p. 363.

[5] Cf. J. A. Bryant, Jr., "Prince Hal and the Ephesians," *Sewanee Review*, LXVII (1959), 204–219; Benjamin T. Spencer, "*2 Henry IV* and the Theme of Time," UTQ, XIII (1944), 394–399.

So shaken as we are, so wan with care,
Find we a time for frighted Peace to pant
And breathe short-winded accents of new broils
To be commenc'd in strands afar remote.
No more the thirsty entrance of this soil
Shall daub her lips with her own children's blood;
No more shall trenching war channel her fields,
Nor bruise her flowerets with the armed hoofs
Of hostile paces. Those opposed eyes,
Which, like the meteors of a troubled heaven,
All of one nature, of one substance bred,
Did lately meet in the intestine shock
And furious close of civil butchery,
Shall now, in mutual well-beseeming ranks,
March all one way and be no more oppos'd
Against acquaintance, kindred, and allies.

(I.i.1–16)

Since the sickness lies solely in civil insurrection, the cure is to be a
simple restoration of national unity, or rather the appearance of unity.
Henry stresses the one nature, one substance of the constituents, the
unnaturalness of civil "butchery," and the attractiveness of a united
body. His rhetoric attempts to embody and make attractive the rigor-
ous, ceremonial order for which he asks. But the diagnosis is shallow
and the appeal, as we eventually learn, partly bogus in that the pro-
posal to engage in a holy war is strategic rather than religious. He
hopes simply to call "Fall in!" and see the chaotic crisscrossing of insurrection and "intestine shock" transformed into "well-beseeming
ranks," all marching one way.

In thinking about the Prince's "riot and dishonour" and his alliance
with Falstaff, Henry reveals almost accidentally that the disturbance
runs deeper. He lapses into the kind of wishful dream that characterizes Richard II:

O that it could be prov'd
That some night-tripping fairy had exchang'd
In cradle-clothes our children where they lay,
And call'd mine Percy, his Plantagenet!

(I.i.86–89)

That he is mistaken about the Prince is perhaps less important than
the indication that the rhetoric of politic calculation is not sufficient to
draw the community, or even the king, together, as Falstaff easily demonstrates. His wish for a different son appears more and more ironic
as we realize that his own "tender conscience" needs a different image

to put on display. But he is not simply trying to avert civil chaos through an appearance of public order; he wants also to *be* something different from himself, the follower of "indirect crook'd ways" to an undeserved crown; and he would like his son, who is really very much his, to be his justification. Obviously, if the Prince turns out to be another Richard, the crooked path will only lead back to the same morass; his public ceremonies will turn out to have been private orgies, held in full view of a commonwealth he thinks should not see too much of a king.

The Hotspur mirror reveals an impulsive drive for self-glorification undermining the community without twinges of conscience. Hotspur in a sense bribes the moral sense by making a religion of chivalric virtues; he discovers or manufactures opponents such as the perfumed "popinjay," Henry, and the Prince, against whom he can legally exercise those virtues. He thinks of heroism as a leaping upward to the pale-faced moon and plunging downward where fathom line could never reach to pluck up maiden-honor, both places suggesting dream fulfillment; but his "vision" is more dynamic than rational. His is an aggressive, individual dream, like those of romance knights, that would make history primarily a chronicle of individual heroic events, incapable of uniting a community except as a collection of followers. (Even so, Hotspur is no further from an adjustment of self and society than John of Lancaster, who has little understanding of personal, subversive tendencies. His strategem at the Forest of Gaultree is justified insofar as Authority needs desperately to keep control, but it cannot, of course, lead to permanent psychic or communal well-being: he submerges the inner self in the machinations of politics, though it reappears now and then, a little strangled, on the surface.)

Falstaff reflects all of these deficiencies, but in a more dangerous form because he has an effective mechanism to handle them. Rather than curing sickness, he explodes tension in laughter, which reconciles us to incongruities without eliminating them. Whereas Hal aims at a comprehensive integration of aggressive and self-transcending tendencies (to borrow Arthur Koestler's terms[6]), Falstaff adjusts to the former —as long as he can—through comic strategies, and grows fat on pretensions to the latter that he sees all around him. The "tragedy" he ultimately faces makes such a static adjustment impossible and forces the audience to abandon it, to reach upward toward some sort of extrapersonal fulfillment. To prevent our substituting resentment for political insight, Shakespeare makes the "tragedy" implicit throughout in the very nature of humor. In Falstaff's first appearance in *1 Henry IV*, for example, though the Prince and Falstaff play lightly with the sub-

---

[6] *Insight and Outlook* (New York, 1949), pp. 57ff.

ject of sickness, the disease goes too deep for purely comic adjustment
or purgation. If hours were indeed "cups of sack, and minutes capons,
and clocks the tongues of bawds, and dials the signs of leaping-houses,
and the blessed sun himself a fair hot wench in flame-coloured taffeta"
(I.ii.7), time would be unredeemable. (The sun image is soon connected
to providential order, an objectively stable and redeemable time, and
the "epiphany" of the new king.) To "go by the moon" as Falstaff pro-
poses, is to lose one's will and become as changeable as the sea; it leads
to an ebb as low as the foot of the ladder and a flow as high "as the
ridge of the gallows" (I.ii.42), not so high as Hotspur plans to leap, but
high enough.

The mock interview is perhaps a clearer example in that the tragic
undertones that prepare the audience to transcend the sea-moon sickness and accept the duties of *Respublica* are more central to the dramatic *agon*. The scene demonstrates the insufficiency of the comic mode
in handling the disturbances of the "times." Whereas comic rebels are
ordinarily animated mannerisms of some kind, or collections of them,
which the dramatist can set in place without destroying, when Falstaff's
"meanings collapse" in absurdity, something besides mannerism and
"make-believe" is lost.[7] The make-believe and the mannerisms are part
of a Falstaffian ceremony of self-creation that Hal is invited to join at
the end of the scene (he has only to concede that his corporeal friend
is more or less permanent). In his failure "to make his body and fur-
nishings mean sovereignty" and thus finally to mean "all the world,"
as Mr. Barber aptly puts it, and in his inability to redeem time through
a private ritual divorced from political and religious duties, Falstaff
himself is destroyed, first symbolically in mock rejection and finally,
of course, in actual "history." The Prince's answer cuts through the
comic facade like a precise surgical instrument. If "each repetition of
'sweet Jack Falstaff, kind Jack Falstaff' aggrandizes an identity which
the serial clauses caress and cherish" (Barber, p. 182), even though
caressing with some irony, the entire structure comes down at the
Prince's sharp pronouncement, "I do, I will." As a kind of official proc-
lamation, his answer expresses not a timeless dream but a present impulse to reject comic ritual and to seek some other adjustment. Though
brief, it has its own rhythm and force; neither self-aggrandizement nor
its protective irony can stand against it.

The sacrificial theme is already explicit at this point and already
rhetorically effective in that we must begin to choose one commitment
in preference to the other, or at least to find some other way to accommodate both. The Prince plans to confront history—which overwhelms
a tragic hero and scarcely involves a comic hero at all—by transcending
the self. And insofar as he takes the audience with him, he makes it

[7] Barber, p. 189.

share his distrust of the ironic ritual of self, as through Hotspur it learns to distrust the dream of personal heroism and through John of Lancaster the suffocation of individual honor in the common will. The Prince's control over impulses of the minute comes primarily through his capacity to see history as a continuous succession of events linking present to past and future. As he learns to control "time," Falstaff more and more loses himself in the present. Living in a timeless, fleeting moment precludes fulfilling future promise, profanes "the precious time," and cuts off the past as a useful, educative force. For to Falstaff, youth is not a time of growth leading continuously to fulfillment; it is adventure, a slim waist, and bells at midnight, seen through a haze of nostalgia (even though that nostalgia can be realistically exploited in others). The present is a rush of officers at the door, interrupting the private life and dragging one off to Shrewsbury. Or it is an attempt to conceal past actions like the performance at Gadshill by recreating them, with changes, in the present—in a sense "mythologizing" them to accommodate self-respect. And the future will be uncertain because if time is essentially a flow of sack, "minutes capons, and clocks the tongues of bawds," absence will be oblivion: "It grows late" (II.iv.299, Part Two). The Prince, on the other hand, in the process of validating the future king's future community, expiates a past curse in the processes of time, experience, and growth. When he gets the best of Falstaff, it is only by connecting past and future as one continuum. Ironically, to do so in the rejection scene, he must make himself appear discontinuous:

> Presume not that I *am* the thing I *was:*
> For God doth know, so shall the world perceive,
> That I have turn'd away my former self;
> So will I those that kept me company.
> When thou dost hear I *am* as *I have been,*
> Approach me, and thou *shalt be* as thou *wast . . .*
> (V.v.60, Part Two)

Falstaff must be made to think he has changed whether he has or not. But Falstaff's blessings would be lost anyway in the essential discontinuity of his own life, in time's always increasing curse: "Thou whoreson little tidy Bartholomew boar-pig," Doll says affectionately, "when wilt thou leave fighting o'days and foining o'nights, and begin to patch up thine old body for heaven?" Falstaff will never be ready for the Totentanz: "Peace, good Doll! do not speak like a death's-head. Do not bid me remember mine end." Which is to say that he attempts to separate present existence from historical continuity, while the Prince submits existence to the controls of honor, duty, public ceremony—in short, social and political tradition.

It is necessity for controls of this kind that makes the sacrifice of Falstaff inevitable. With this in mind, we might think of the history play as a dramatic demonstration of how to counter the disintegrative and antisocial impulses of self through a sense of continuous historical "transcendence." Such transcendence does not necessarily involve freedom from time and the demands of ego—Hal accepts past guilt and future duties, and is personally ambitious—but with some qualifications, as we shall see later, it puts such demands in a meaningful historical framework that liberates hero and audience from any particular demand: a moment in history is less overpowering when connected in sequence with what has passed and what is to come.

Some of the limitations of the function of Falstaff's "tragedy" in the series are implicit in this stress on continuity and tradition. The province of the history play is not the inner world or the world of fable but a historical world like the one outside the theater, engrossed in politics and asking that taxes be paid. Its hero never quite escapes into legend or touches the deepest layers of our sympathy. It is concerned with the redemptive virtues, or lack of them, and leaves unexplored the more absorbing depths of individual motivation that ordinarily occupy tragedy. For this reason, Falstaff's "tragic" slavery to time, like his comic absurdity, is perhaps best interpreted as simply a failure in historical vision, a failure in adjustment to "history." The history play, through its hero or exposure of non-heroes, shows the audience how to make that adjustment.

II

Not until his public denunciation of Falstaff does the Prince become the manifest center of community tradition. Before the redemptive process reaches that completion, he must undergo several trials— against Hotspur and the sick king as well as against Falstaff—all of which force him to rise above himself as an apparent rioter-in-time and become someone the world can "perceive," who is without discrepancy between inner self and outer act. As he helps defeat the rebels, he takes over their powers in the manner of a morality-play hero and consigns to the grave their unredeemable qualities—the hidden conspiracies, inner guilt, and aggressive egoism—which cause discontinuity in both personal life and public tradition. At each step he thus becomes more clearly the purified and evident "continuator" who will assume the inherited crown and weld, after his epiphany, an unbroken chain of order from God to man, past to future. (Quelling political rebellion, of course, is but one of the purgative acts.[8]) In the deaths of both Hotspur and the king, the transfer and purgation which make that chain possible are explicit:

> *Prince.* . . . And all the budding honours on thy crest
> I'll crop, to make a garland for my head. (V.iv.71)

> *King.* . . . God knows, my son
> By what by-paths and indirect crook'd ways
> I met this crown; . . .
> To thee it shall descend with better quiet,
> Better opinion, better confirmation;
> For all the soil of the achievement goes
> With me into earth. (IV.v.184ff., Part Two)

> *King [Henry V].* My father is gone wild into his grave
> For in his tomb lie my affections;
> And with spirit sadly I survive,
> To mock the expectation of the world,
> To frustrate prophecies, and to raze out
> Rotten opinion, who hath writ me down
> After my seeming. (V.ii.123, Part Two)

The discontinuity between son and father can be resolved completely only when the son becomes father and casts off his childhood, or sublimates its Oedipal impulses, or whatever, on behalf of the "fatherland." Feelings toward the state as a kind of super-parent—the "womb of kings" and the fatherland all in one—are much less ambivalent than those toward the king-father. Hence, as the "soil" of the king's achievement is buried, the Prince's own "offending" qualities are purged. As Canterbury recalls in *Henry V,*

> Consideration like an angel came
> And whipp'd th' offending Adam out of him,
> Leaving his body as a paradise
> T' envelop and contain celestial spirits.
> (I.i.28)

Canterbury is less than critical of the Prince's strategy, but "consideration's" final banishment of prodigality is clearly to be taken as a purification, the full effects of which are revealed only in *Henry V.* Time and death, which defeat Falstaff, sanctify the lineal descent, wash the blood from the inherited crown, and establish the Prince as vicegerent of cosmic stability.

---

[8] Hugh Dickinson oversimplifies the redemptive process, I think, in pinning it entirely on the defeat of Percy. See "The Reformation of Prince Hal," SQ, XII (1961), 33–46.

The rebellious spirit dies differently in each case, but the same general process holds true: in each *agon* the Prince gains tighter control of the "intestine shocks" that disturb both the individual and the nation. In the psychomachian battle of Shrewsbury, Shakespeare brings together the main rebels of Part One and has the Prince collect his honors. The insurrectionists appear misled and willfully blind. Douglas, for example, attacks various false images of the king and supposes Falstaff to be dead. (The Prince is misled in a different way: his address to the "dead" friend is a stylized and symbolic rejection rather than a comic mistake that discredits him.) From these acts, we surmise that Douglas does not have his finger on either the national or the individual pulse. Though in both cases he admittedly has reason for confusion, he cannot tell a true king or a live man. The persistent reappearance of the "kings" suggests that the rightful government is omnipresent and a bit mystifying to the outsider. Despite his huffing and puffing, the House of Lancaster refuses to come down and Falstaff, thinking reluctantly of reforming, springs back up again. Rebellion can do nothing but fly headlong "upon the foot of fear." As the entire fabric of self-seeking masquerading as public interest and moral indignation collapses, history appears to have justified the "crook'd ways" and reformed the rioters.

Once we grant the peculiar way the folk hero has of expelling antitypes and absorbing their strength, we are less likely to dispute the Prince's capacity at Shrewsbury to assume Hotspur's chivalric prowess or, in Part Two, his right to acquire his father's political acuteness. That Henry V likewise absorbs something of Falstaff is more difficult to demonstrate. I think, however, that in a sense the new king has learned from Falstaff. To be sure, the Prince's avowed pretexts for plucking the "base strings" would not indicate a profound educational process; and when he thinks Falstaff dead, his grief is significantly qualified by the disenchanting remark, "O, I should have a heavy miss of thee / If I were much in love with vanity!" which substitutes a contrary-to-fact conditional for regret. (If the lines are spoken as a kind of ritual disclaimer, encomium would be out of place and perhaps suggest that Hal's "I do, I will" was not seriously intended after all.) As a final, apparently gratuitous, insult he threatens to have Falstaff "embowell'd" to suit him for lying beside "noble Percy," which may seem to de-Falstaff what is left (though Falstaff is listening, of course, which makes that threat, too, a mixture of comic and tragic foreboding).

But if the strategy of the history play is to convince the audience that nothing is lost in the state's relentless pursuit of its Manifest Destiny, even sacrifices must pay dividends. Falstaff's vitality must not be entirely lost. It is less easily transferred than Percy's chivalry and the sick king's power, but like these it must be made continuous if it is to survive; its "body" must be made less, its "grace" more. In a sense, then, it is left for *Henry V* to demonstrate the validity of the sacrifices required during the course of the Henry IV plays and *Richard II*, which first began shattering dream worlds in the interest of efficient government: the slaying of individual impulses and anarchistic dreams is justified only if public action makes self-fulfillment possible in some other way. Henry V as a public figure thus becomes very central to the series of plays. The audience must have a protagonist of some dimension, both human and "public," to make the center of its circle. The shell of tradition without inner life is no more binding than the verbal observance of love that Lear forces upon his daughters.

Shakespeare has no trouble making Henry V transcend Hotspur, Henry IV, and himself as truant Prince. Though he has been a comparatively passive and shifting figure at Gadshill and Eastcheap, merely the chief knight at Shrewsbury, and an outsider at the Forest of Gaultree, in *Henry V* he becomes the center and wholesale manipulator of the action. Beyond that, on a few occasions his coolness of judgment and his hot quest for honor are animated by a comparatively high degree of vitality and humanity. I suspect that Shakespeare meant to suggest *vestigia Falstaffi* in places other than the dialogue of Pistol and the Hostess, which is designed to lay to rest whatever miscellaneous emotions might still be getting in the way. The shrewdness, expediency, and courage which Henry has taken from his father and Hotspur are significantly altered in the composite character of the new king, not by what Falstaff has taught him directly, but by what Falstaff represents. Irony and humor have been suppressed because, as we have seen, these lead to a static adjustment of aggressive tendencies rather than to reform and heroic action. The jest of the tennis balls Henry turns into a provocation for war, or pretends to; the practical joke he sets in motion on the eve of battle he drains of humor the next day, when the king must appear king. But some of the vitality of Eastcheap and Gadshill remains. Henry unites realistic pragmatism, ability to accommodate personal impulses quickly to difficult situations, and the bearing of a man-among-men. In doing so he rises above the average patrician and the inflexible professional hero.

Whatever he might have learned from Eastcheap, Henry seems clearly meant to illustrate the highest potentials of the active life. Even his coldbloodedness can work two ways: it may be an operation of pure, disinterested intelligence taking calculated risks, or it may embrace alternatives and choose the right one out of a comprehensive moral perspective, impossible without some degree of humanity. Spiritual energy is clearly part of his impelling force—though this does not mean that he cannot be shrewd at the same time. In handling the treachery of Cambridge, Grey and Scroop, to choose a representative exampie, he is compassionate as well as crafty. Meeting calculation with calculation, he brings the three conspirators to an unavoidable moral recognition and finally to contrition. Though the transformation may seem unbelievable in psychological terms, the idea of shifting the burden of execution to the conspirators themselves is scarcely reprehensible in itself. In the context of the play, they are responsible for their inner values in the same way that soldiers are for their souls upon entering battle: Henry insists that maintaining fine distinctions between what belongs to the community and what is one's own is necessary to the health of both individual and state. Considering the "kingdom's safety" he believes to be the king's first duty; to act more mercifully, as again in the execution of Bardolph, would be softhearted cruelty (III.vi.115). *Given the conspiracy to begin with,* repentance is the highest good salvageable.

Henry thus finds personal fulfillment in the "office" rather than in self-definition. The "affection" which Bradley finds in short supply in him, he reserves for this "happy few, [this] band of brothers"—with himself at the head, of course. But Shakespeare, in the Henry plays at least, does not imply that being public in this way requires sacrificing the "citadel of absolute truth, the inner self." [9] Although it is not difficult to diminish the king by measuring him against later tragic protagonists, he is not without virtues. Seen strictly from the standpoint of adjustment of polity, he compares favorably with other Shakespearian heroes: beside him, Coriolanus is an ego-maniac, Caesar an impostor, Antony unscrupulous (in one play) and weak (in the other), and Brutus confused; even Hamlet, as a Prince, appears unbalanced, deprived by the sickness of his world of shaping the state to his inherent magnanimity. After the tragic hero has departed with the sickness and strength of his egoism upon him, Shakespeare ordinarily has a public figure such as Malcolm or Fortinbras reassemble the scattered energies of the community and give it coherence and historical duration. Personal isolation and the shattering of communal bonds he shows to be consequences of seeking too intently the "citadel of absolute truth." Henry is not so destructive or so interesting as that, but his limitations do not necessarily indicate that "Falstaff wins after all."

What they do indicate is not easy to determine, but if we were to ignore them we would tend to make an historic epic of some sort out of an historic drama. It may be that Shakespeare is realistic about the king simply to show the irrelevance of personal flaws in the fully absorbing center of community emotion. The intensity of the myth can be measured by the amount of reality it supports without collapsing, which in Shakespeare can be a good deal. In Henry's case, the myth is

[9] Ellis-Fermor, p. 54.

reinforced by the authorical chorus and by imagistic patterns and
echoes from scripture suggesting an analogy between divine and temporal order. The mirror of Christian kings *in his way* is the mirror of
the Christian King: the action of redeeming time imitates the Redemption; the epiphany of the new king imitates the Epiphany; the hierar-
chal structure of the kingdom imitates cosmic structure. Henry's imitation remains imperfect because the history play, unlike mystery or
morality plays, remains essentially indeterminate. But despite these
limitations, Henry as folk hero fuses a diversity of individual impulses
into a unified, social organism that is more than the sum of uses one
segment makes of another.

The pre-battle speech (IV.iii.18) reveals something of how the fusion
is accomplished. (Since it is long and familiar, I shall not quote it.) We
know from the nighttime dialogues that the king does not ignore the
dangers he has put his subjects in, but neither does he allow responsibility to paralyze him. The hard-headed plainness, the blunt wit, and
the colloquial idiom of the wooing scene are evident before he reaches
the drawing room. We know, too, how far democratic instincts have
penetrated, without destroying, distinctions of rank and social level.
The main point here is that his rhetoric, despite its hortative battlefield simplicity, catches all of this in its net. It uses but goes beyond
the Hotspurian logic of chivalry and the policy involved in rousing the
troops at a crucial moment. The repetition is less mechanical, less calculated than Bolingbroke's, which plays upon the emotions without
emotion through an intellectual balance of clauses and a manufactured
pattern of images and figures. Henry, like Falstaff in the mock-rejec-
tion scene, obviously enjoys words which name and glorify tangible
objects close to the center of his self-interest; he savors the names which
when sounded in the future will continue to weld into a brotherhood
those who were initiated at Agincourt. The difference between his
rhetoric of names and Falstaff's ritual is that the former creates a group
myth, the latter sanctifies the person and personality of the speaker; one
looks forward and the other magnifies the present. But both are adept
at word-magic. They add communion to communication, in Allen
Tate's phrase, and thus avoid a dehumanized rhetoric that reveals
nothing of the inner self and leaves even vital community interests
untouched.

Henry's speech is partly a wishful dream of heroism but is unques-
tionably alive and realistic. It is thus well suited to the form and purpose of the history play. Like the total action, it argues for the sacrifice of personal life in a communal act which will repay the men "with
advantages"—provided, of course, that they believe in the king. It is a
national version of finding selfhood by losing it, to be sealed by the
ritual of bloodshed which makes all men equal, "gentling" those to

whom the king has talked in the darkness and who in no tangible political or economic sense will ever be raised.

In the history play, the function of an "epic" speech such as this is to redeem those times that can imaginatively share in the myth: to shape the present so that men "in their flowing cups," "yearly on the vigil feast," will remember the myth. For such history, Shakespeare implies, is never remote to an audience held by the "muse of fire"; relived in the theater, it will make a nationalistic group once again a "band of brothers." [10] Henry is probably meant to be justified both in envying the peasant's "best advantages" and in doing everything in his power to secure his grasp on the crown, even though preventing civil turmoil entails a foreign war. To withdraw from responsibility is impossible, or at least risky, as Lear discovers: to assume it without reservation will violate some things, strengthen others. Pursuing a course inherently contaminating, Henry never quite loses equilibrium or allows public obligations to reduce inner life to mechanism.

III

The process of purified absorption undoubtedly has less tangible aspects also. Folk heroes acquire powers, as they mount horses, differently from public school boys:

> I saw young Harry with his beaver on,
> His cuisses on his thighs, gallantly arm'd
> Rise from the ground like feathered Mercury,
> And vaulted with such ease into his seat
> As if an angel dropp'd down from the clouds
> To turn and wind a fiery Pegasus
> And witch the world with noble horsemanship.
>   (IV.i.104ff., Part One)

(That a rider's control of his mount was a common figure for the soul's control of its body explains away some but not all of the witch-

---

[10] The levels of awareness in an audience thus told that it would re-enact what it was in fact re-enacting must have been complex. One of the functions of the Chorus, which provides an unusually elaborate mediation between playwright, audience, and play, is to sharpen awareness of the play as play. The Olivier film version carries the point even further. At the conclusion, "Henry" is suddenly revealed as the actor-who-has-been-king: the "performance" is over and the myth shrinks back into present reality. And since the film begins from a perspective outside the Globe and circles in upon the action, there is a further movement from the Shakesperian to the modern theater. The Elizabethan golden age has been part of the myth; and so the modern audience, finding itself outside both the community of the old king and the world of 1599, must make a double "adjustment." The film becomes not so much an apology for *Respublica* as distant history in two layers.

ing skill.) Despite the suggestions of superhuman power in the king, however, Shakespeare's dramatic method in presenting him is at least as close to realism as to the technique of the morality and miracle plays. "Participation" in the communal emotion centered in the king results not only from the king's mythological stature and incantational rhetoric but also from a realistic examination of alternatives in various counter-actions or dialectical "plots" that close off other channels.

The attempt to turn "disease" to commodity is one of these counter-actions. Nearly everyone in the series from *Richard II* to *Henry V* at one time or another thinks of exploiting the weakness of the realm or of other parties in it, partly by conjuring the right spirits and partly by simple political trickery. In *2 Henry IV*, the rebels, having been "o'erset," venture again; the Archbishop of York "turns insurrection to religion" and attempts to capitalize upon "a bleeding land,/Gasping for life" (I.ii.207); Northumberland lies, as Rumour says, "crafty sick," awaiting a time to emerge and redeem his honor when the state seems weak enough to allow it. Falstaff is again the key figure, of course. If he comes on stage asking about time in Part One, in Part Two he appears inquiring about his ailing health and advanced age, both equally beyond fixing but not beyond "use." "A man can no more separate age and covetousness than 'a can part young limbs and lechery," he rationalizes; "the gout galls the one, and the pox pinches the other"; but a "good wit will make use of anything. I will turn diseases to commodity" (I.ii.256,277). His inability to do so is the source of both comedy and tragedy, as we have seen. Desire, outliving performance, becomes grotesque, like the clawing of poll by parrot, in the Prince's figure. The pressure of time is unbalancing, as a note of desperation comes into the Eastcheap follies. Hostess Quickly chants imperatively to Doll (who also turns disease to commodity): "O, run, Doll, run; run, good Doll. Come. (*She comes blubbered.*) Yea, will you come, Doll?" (II.iv.420, Part Two).

The emphasis upon commodity is one side of Falstaff's partly real and partly mock gentleman-capitalist role, which complements his Puritanism. He is a "robber" both of "pilgrims going to Canterbury with rich offerings" and of "traders riding to London with fat purses" (I.ii.140). As Gadshill observes, he goes with "burgomasters" who "pray continually to their saint, the commonwealth; or rather, not pray to her, but prey on her" (II.i.87). His expenses, though hardly frugal, are itemized. Shakespeare apparently attaches this cluster of middle-class values to the aristocrat in order to purge them along with other things that "offend." After Falstaff's death, an increased acquisitiveness characterizes his old group, as it slips further and further toward the periphery of the legitimate community. Pistol *owns* Quickly and advises Nym to get papers on Doll as fast as possible (II.i.

77): "My Love," he commands the Hostess, "give me thy lips./Look
to my chattels and my moveables" (II.iii.49). He plans to sell pro-
visions to the army and thus acquire whatever profits war will afford
(II.i.116). Falstaff had at least held upper and lower levels together;
now that he is dead, Pistol says, "we must earn" (II.iii.5), that is, both
"grieve" and make a living.[11] And "earning" as they do leads to petty
thievery, even to the gallows.

Shakespeare thus minimizes the kind of bourgeois communal power
that economic bonds have in Heywood, Dekker, and other middle-
class dramatists. But the spiritual bonds of the medieval community
have also weakened, and any dramatist interested in more than individual profit motives must do something with the Goddess Utility on
a social scale. Hence Henry, like the Bastard, is made aware of lost
spiritual bonds and the power of commodity—a money-minded church
plays easily into his hands—but he substitutes for them chivalric and
heroic virtues, by and large, rather than middle-class virtues. Because
the motives behind Falstaff's desire to turn disease to commodity are
primarily egoistic and unheroic, he rejects them and turns to the old
framework of higher virtues. (After the Histories, Shakespeare will
place "chivalry" in a tragic environment and show it to be dis-
integrating. Someone like Edmund who has violated the old hier-
archies and grown possessive will usually give the death blow. Its
potential weakness is already clear in *1 Henry IV* when Hotspur
momentarily becomes acquisitive and makes the rebellion—supposedly
on behalf of honor—look dangerously like a land grab.) The Henry
plays explore the profit motive thoroughly, however, in return sub-
jecting the heroic virtues to Falstaff's utilitarian wit. That honor and
criticism of his "betters" should be Falstaff's steady diet is an indication that rank and the chivalric distinctions it is based on can now be
threatened from below, as *Richard II* discovers, without flights of

[11] The economic aspects of Pistol's "earning" are reinforced by his speech a few
lines later:

> Look to my chattels and my movables.
> Let senses rule; the word is "Pitch and Pay."
> Trust none;
> For oaths are straws, men's faiths are wafercakes,
> And hold-fast is the only dog, my duck. . . .
> Let us to France; like horse-leeches, my boys,
> To suck, to suck, the very blood to suck!
>   (II.iii.50)

Rather than ritualizing theft as Falstaff had in his role as Saturnalian king, Pistol
turns from ritual—the elegy for Falstaff—to economic "blood-sucking." (The pun
on "earn" is the pivot.) And whereas Falstaff's game had attracted and educated the
young Prince, the serious business of Pistol and his group cannot hold the "boy,"
who finally seeks out "some better service" (III.ii.54). The counter-action has lost
its dialectical, Saturnalian function.

angels coming to their defense. A king who has taken the crown expediently must be especially aware of "what the people are saying": the new freedom to climb entails an increasing danger of falling. Public life on all levels, from Iago-like disputes over status and promotion to the politics of a Coriolanus, is a different and more complicated concern.

Falstaff, of course, with his easy movement among levels—from Eastcheap taverns to pre-battle councils—and his threat to make the Prince a career robber of the king's treasury, is a champion of anti-chivalric flexibility. If it takes a war to "gentle" the lowly, wit levels kings without stirring from the chair. In turning disease to commodity, he attacks more than the economic order, however; he also translates moral distinctions downward to purely physical phenomena, and in doing so indirectly affirms the relentless natural law to which he eventually falls. Commodity and naturalism are closely linked in him, as in Edmund. Though the links are made with more wit than cunning, beneath the humor the way is continually being prepared for the king's comment, "know the grave doth gape/For thee thrice wider than for other men," a caustic remark that only recapitulates what Falstaff himself has implied:

> *Ch. Just.* Well, the truth is, Sir John, you live in great infamy.
> *Fal.* He that buckles himself in my belt cannot live in less.
> *Ch. Just.* Your means are very slender, and your waste is great.
> *Fal.* I would it were otherwise; I would my means were greater, and my waist slenderer. (I.ii.156, Part Two)

Through the puns Falstaff tries to convert moral disease to mere physical disproportion, which seems the lesser sin—until the Prince suggests that the wider the "grave" for those "surfeit-swell'd," the less the "grace." His last attempt to convert disease to commodity in working Justice Shallow for a thousand pounds carries him rushing into disaster; ironically, he goes to "cure" the young king, "sick" for him, by taking him for what he can.

In "observingly" distilling his experience, the Prince, too, turns disease to commodity, but differently. What he takes from the public till he repays, and what he takes from his antitypes would have been lost or misused anyway. Theoretically, there is nothing at fault with the strategy provided it is made subject to moral controls. Warwick describes it quite accurately when he remarks that

> The Prince but studies his companions
> Like a strange tongue, wherein, to gain the language,
> 'Tis needful that the most immodest word
> Be look'd upon and learn'd; . . .
>   So, like gross terms,

The Prince will in the perfectness of time
Cast off his followers; and their memory
Shall as a pattern or a measure live,
By which his Grace must mete the lives of others,
Turning past evils to advantages. (IV.iv.67ff., Part Two)

Thus even Falstaff serves the kingdom "in the perfectness of time"—
that is, in the perfection of time redeemed by the new king—because
past evils, or evil of any kind, can be turned to advantage by the
scrupulously unscrupulous. Thus Henry V can play upon the acquisitive instinct without being corrupted by it. His kind of expediency rejects, but with open eyes, the ways which many realists in the
audience knew of "getting ahead."

IV

We can now return to the rejection scene, which brings together
many of the aspects of the history play we have observed, and see it
from either "character" or "ritualistic" criticism. If equilibrium between self and society is indeed achieved in it, we should expect to
find Falstaff's "death" appearing inevitable; it should serve to unite
the community in the theater, as in the play, by ridding it of the
egocentrism that has crystallized around Falstaff and his ways of con-
fronting time, seeking commodity, curing disease, and so forth. The
rejection scene is the first time, of course, that Falstaff is aware that
a tutor and feeder of riots is unwelcome in court. His recognition is
thus nicely timed to coincide with and contribute to the final manifestation of the king and the *anagnorisis* of the audience. His defen-
sive masks are stripped off and he is suddenly faced with the blatant
fact of public life. His heart, Pistol says, is "fracted and corroborate,"
which is partly humorous and partly pathetic; it is "killed by the
King."

The slayer-king speaks not only as an ex-truant but also as the
exemplar of psychological order. Falstaff's appeal, "My king! my Jove!
I speak to thee, my heart!" recognizes that the "head" of the temporal
order functions on at least three levels simultaneously, as king, Jove,
and heart of his subjects; he speaks with the rhetoric of elevated
majesty, personal teacher, and last judge.[12] It is significant that the
first time we are fully convinced of the unity of Hal's impulses and
the wholeness of his character, he is playing his most complex role:
he cannot *be* himself until he is king. The disjunction in his former

[12] See Harold Jenkins, *The Structural Problem in Shakespeare's Henry the Fourth*
(London, 1956), p. 14.

life as a rioter under bond to promise is healed by making the promise reality and by consigning the rest to unreal dream. The discrepancy between present and past appearance has never "really" existed, however, for he *is* the thing he *was*, even if not the thing Falstaff and the kingdom took him to be. His educational process has added to his essential character but not disturbed its underlying continuity.

But the chief dramatic point would seem to be that Shakespeare refuses to negotiate the loss of Falstaff, as Bradley wishes he had (p. 253). The language is harsh because *under the circumstances* it could not have been dramatically effective otherwise: the realities of time and disease which the play has made important must be confronted without evasion, conservatism being more deeply ingrained in the play than Falstaff. Thus, though comedy could not expel "such a kind of man" with a clear conscience, history must contrive to get along without him. If we expect a purely tragic "resolution," however, we shall not be quite prepared for what we receive. Falstaff is too human to be dealt with like Malvolio but not of high enough stature for pure tragedy. The rejection scene lacks the kind of language that could transform the unpleasant "fact" to cathartic poetry, nor does it attempt to do so entirely. The community must be made a charmed circle through another kind of rhetoric, part public speech and part confession, flexible, direct, and capable of embracing reality freed from the "long dream."

Difficulties besides that of the language are involved also. The history play must be plotted so as to satisfy our sense of form as though it had beginning, middle, and end, and yet must somehow be left open. Its subject matter leads to plays in a series rather than to single, self-contained works, and even the series cannot be decisively ended. In the tragical histories, Shakespeare emphasizes the new reign, or England's possibilities if it "to itself do rest but true," or the new unity between "the white rose and the red." In the rejection scene, he divides attention about equally between the promising community surrounding the new king and the "catastrophe" of personal life.[13] The result is a kind of *concordia discors;* to borrow Canterbury's words, heaven divides

---

[13] Public duty and private impulse are not "represented" in Hal and Falstaff as in an allegory, of course. If the Prince absorbs some of Falstaff, Falstaff in turn picks up a Lancastrian political device or two. He is well aware of the figure he and his companions will cut when arraigned before the emerging king, for example. Even their tattered clothes he will turn to advantage, appearing "to seem stained with travel and sweating with desire to see him; thinking of nothing else, putting all affairs else in oblivion, as if there were nothing else to be done but to see him" (V.v.24). We know that the "as if" is justified and that even with Falstaff friendship and patronage go hand in hand: "woe to my Lord Chief Justice" and "Blessed are they that have been my friends."

78   *Harold E. Toliver*

> The state of man in divers functions,
> Setting endeavour in continual motion;
> To which is fixed, as an aim or butt,
> Obedience. (*Henry V*, I.ii.185ff.)

But even such formulas as this are not completely "fixed"; they must be tested continually against the circumstances of history. (For this reason I have used the word "adjustment" rather than "reconcilement" or "resolution.") Rather than concluding things once and for all, the history play ends at a plateau or brief breathing space from which the state looks backward with relief but forward with apprehension. Even the glories of Henry V, as the audience knew, were to wither in the continued curse of Henry VI and Richard III. (Despite the apparently romantic-comedy ending of *Henry V*, Shakespeare goes out of the way to recall the future.) And it is doubtful that Elizabethans felt collectively and spontaneously that somehow Elizabeth had fixed mutability once and for all.

The best that 2 *Henry IV* can do is make its auditors participants in a historical ceremony which frees them from the gormandizing dream without robbing them of their individual wills. It demands "obedience" but not an absolute regimentation of "diverse functions" and endeavors set "in continual motion." Shakespeare will have his squire of the night's body—and thus the dark, protected center of self-interest—and not have him either, if he can transubstantiate part of him; and failing that, he would not likely suffer so much from the incongruity of loving and hating the same man as modern readers might, who are that much further from gothic ambivalences: who have never experienced the weird illogic of the moralities, which award the official palm to Order and make us remember Riot. He would probably not hesitate, in other words, to choose Order, with whatever ritual can be put in it, over an instinctive anarchy insufficiently protected from the world by its comic strategies. And when we consider that such "magic" as Henry performs in redeeming time —and thus as Shakespeare performs in redeeming history—is effective without demanding that we accept simply on faith the night-tripping "elfin guardians," [14] we can perhaps avoid adding new levels to the schizophrenic feeling for Falstaff. It is not a question of either swallowing duty, sweetly covered with ritual, or rebelling on behalf of all that Falstaff stands for—and feeling dissatisfied in either case: the community which the history play imitates has its own legitimate life.

As to the form of that imitation, we can perhaps let Morgann have

---

[14] Cf. A. P. Rossiter's statement in *Woodstock: A Moral History* (London, 1946), "magic is part of the Tudor world, not least where Monarchy is touched" (p. 12).

the last word; for in his role as pre-romantic critic, he leaves room both for the categories into which we put dramatic types and for the unique, organic form by which a given play "takes in" its audience, sometimes in defiance of normal expectations and tendencies to favor certain elements. He has Aristotle (surprisingly) rebuke such critics-by-generic-rule as Thomas Rhymer who expect the old categories to hold true for all times: "True poesy is *magic*," Aristotle admonishes, "not *nature;* an effect from causes hidden or unknown. To the magician I prescribed no laws; his law and his power are one; his power is his law." Shakespeare, seeing something even in a king who remains alive at the end of the play, made new laws of genre to accommodate him.

The Final Scenes of 2 *Henry IV*

by Derek Traversi

The last scenes, indeed, lead each in its own way to the final
rejection. The first, as though to anticipate the return of the Lord
Chief Justice, shows us something of the local application of the
law as opposed to the grandeur of the abstract principle upon which
royalty itself is to rest, admitting the necessity of its restraining
power. The Gloucestershire of Justice Shallow, indeed, has been conceived from the first as a reflection, a kind of petty microcosm of
the surrounding world. As in England itself, authority, placed in
the enfeebled hands of its age-stricken representative, totters on the
brink of impotence and becomes—not less than the royal office in its
more extensive sphere—the prey to conflicting intrigues, pursued in
the first place by his own servants and supremely, with a greater and
more consistent self-awareness, by Falstaff.

Justice, in fact, as Shallow exercises it, is close, narrow and mean
in the defence of petty interests—as in the decision to "stop . . . William's wages about the sack he lost the other day at Hinckley fair"
—ungenerous in its treatment of those below and aware, in its
senility, of the need to propitiate "appetite," when it is believed that
"appetite," in the person of Falstaff, has the ear of authority: "I will
use him well: a friend i' the court is better than a penny in purse."
Davy, Shallow's servant, is in turn a hanger-on of the local power,
which he seeks to use for his own ends. To further these, he asks his
master to "countenance" William Visor against Clement Perkes "of
the hill," in spite of his admitted roguery. The grounds of his plea
for the "knave" amount, on their own petty level, to an inversion
of the impartiality of justice:

> An honest man, sir, is able to speak for himself, when a knave is not.
> I have served your worship truly, sir, this eight years; and if I cannot
> once or twice in a quarter bear out a knave against an honest man,

I have but a very little credit with your worship. The knave is mine honest friend, sir.

(V.i)

Once more, the last word is left, in a spirit now openly cynical, to Falstaff. Between Shallow and his men there is, he says, "a semblable coherence"; for

they, by observing of him, do bear themselves like foolish justices; he, by conversing with them, is turned into a justice-like serving-man: their spirits are so married in conjunction with the participation of society that they flock together in consent, like so many wild-geese.

(V.i)

This, observed by one outside all forms and restraints of society, is the picture of an England which this play consistently represents as old and corrupt, where power and "appetite" reign unchecked, and where the naked reality of each is only partly transformed respectively in the forms of royal authority and free human energy. The Falstaff of this play is shrewd enough to see things as they are, and not as convention would have them be; but, having so seen them, he is ready to ascribe to them a propensity to evil, invincible in man— "It is certain that either wise bearing or ignorant carriage is caught, as men take diseases, one of another"—and, beyond this, to turn them into jest: "I will devise matter enough out of this Shallow to keep Prince Harry in continual laughter the wearing out of six fashions, which is four terms." Here, however, he overreaches himself. The Henry whom he will soon meet for the last time is no longer in a mood to be kept in "continual laughter" by those who formerly amused him. Believing fundamentally in nothing, except perhaps in the comic energy which is now failing him, Falstaff is confident enough to suppose that his wit can impose itself indefinitely, dominating society in the light of his own nihilism and to his own advantage; and this pride, which has long outlived any validity which his former vital energy may have conferred upon it, is the prelude to his fall.

The following scene at last brings Henry, now about to be crowned, face to face with the personal embodiment of the justice upon which his power will rest. It returns, in other words, to the *public* issues, in which Falstaff has no part and which he has throughout repudiated. After the opening expressions of foreboding by the Lord Chief Justice and the younger princes, Henry appears "attended," no longer Prince Hal, as we have hitherto known him, in some sense now less a man than a symbol of the majesty of power demanding the reverence by which alone—it seems—anarchy can

be avoided. His first speech, for all the deliberate intent to set his
hearers at ease—

> Not Amurath an Amurath succeeds,
> But Harry Harry.

—confirms the new situation. From now on, Henry is a public
figure, consecrated to the royalty he has assumed; and even natural
grief has become for him a garment to be worn, not, indeed, in
insincerity, but in the light of a vocation in terms of which no
emotion can be purely private or personal:

> Sorrow so royally in you appears
> That I will deeply *put the fashion on*
> And wear it in my heart.

This heart, though capable no doubt of true feeling, is now a
"public" heart, dedicated to the austere necessities of a great office;
and, as the spirit of the assertion balances true emotion—"deeply"—
so the final reassurance, rather than resting on personal sentiment
alone, looks forward to the exercise of the royal vocation:

> weep that Harry's dead; and so will I;
> But Harry lives, that shall convert these tears
> By number into hours of happiness.

Henry, as king, can say what might, in Harry the son, have appeared
presumptuous; for the man is now being assumed into the monarch,
the private into the public figure, and the father's desire to con-
ciliate his rivals is from now on assumed into the son's determination
to lead his country in unity and concord.

The two central speeches of the scene convey a second public
"conversion" to correspond to the first, already revealed in his reconciliation to his father. They have, without doubt, their value,
indispensable to this political conception; but, when due weight
has been given to this, it is hard to feel that the dramatist's principal
interest lies here, or that the Lord Chief Justice occupies a central
place in this series of plays, or can be described as a sufficient counterpart to the "riot" incarnated in Falstaff. In accordance with the inherited theme, the Lord Chief Justice stresses his position as the
"image" of the royal power, and insists upon the dependence of rule
itself on a proper respect for the sanctions he embodies. The argument
is a weighty one, for behind it lies the fear of chaos so close to the
Elizabethan mind (and not least to Shakespeare's own), the repudia-
tion of an "appetite" that, once allowed free play, would

> spurn at your most royal image
> And mock your workings in a second body.

Weighty as it is, however, it is a *political* argument, and as such its advocate advances it. Personal considerations have little room for expression here and indeed, when the Lord Chief Justice calls on Henry to imagine himself as king confronted, like his father before him, with a rebellious son, there is a deliberate frigidity about his assertion of the judicial function from which we may feel that personal feeling has been excluded:

> Behold yourself so by a son disdain'd;
> And then imagine me taking your part
> And in your power soft silencing your son:
> After this cold considerance, sentence me.
>
> (V.ii)

The appeal is to the king in his public function, in which "cold" consideration is needed, not to the presumptive father in his affection; and in the exercise of just power, "soft silencing" the rebellion of his own blood, the emphasis is on impersonal severity rather than upon human bonds of unity. The Chief Justice, in other words, though he belongs beyond doubt to the political framework on which this play, and its predecessors, rest, is barely touched by the currents of more intimate feeling that animate its finest episodes; and in this division between public theme and private emotion, politics and humanity, we may sense the presence of some of the deepest inspiration of these plays.

The king, in his reply, assumes the impersonal function required of him. His obeisance, confirming the renunciation of his past, is to the "bold, just and impartial spirit" with which justice needs to be exercised if it is to raise itself above faction and civil strife. Once again the emphasis is on the "public" essence of the royal function. *Publicly*, Henry announces his determination to "stoop and humble" his intents to "your well-practised wise directions," to what is, in effect, less a moral conception than one of policy and practical wisdom; though in saying this one does not assert the practice of deceit, but rather of a necessary Machiavellism, as essential to the conception. The gesture of acceptance having been made, as befits a king who is renouncing not only his unruly past, but, in some sense, his free impulses, the speech rises to a firm affirmation of self-control, as impressive as it is curiously strained, emptied of normal feeling:

> The tide of blood in me
> Hath proudly flow'd in vanity till now:
> Now doth it turn and ebb back to the sea,
> Where it shall mingle with the state of floods
> And flow henceforth in formal majesty.

This is an assertion of moral power rather than of human understanding. Behind the image of the tide so impressively evoked, there is a sense of the various resources of man turned, harnessed to an end, which is the end of "formal majesty." This conception prepares us, once Falstaff has been finally rejected, for the spirit of Henry V.

Before the rejection, however, the background, at once comic and sombre, of the real England of this play returns in two short, but telling scenes (V.iii and iv). The first shows Falstaff at a pretence of merry-making with Shallow and his companions in Gloucestershire: Falstaff flattering the victim whose senility he hopes to turn to profit —it is now " 'Fore God, you have here a goodly dwelling and a rich" —and Shallow accepting the flattery and yet turning it, with the disillusionment that goes with age, to a sense of vanity: "Barren, barren, barren: beggars all, beggars all, Sir John." The opposition of emotional motives—Silence's senile effort at mildly dissolute songs in memory of his lost youth, Falstaff's ironic comment, "I did not think Master Silence had been a man of this mettle," the last faint echo of "Riot" which is itself a sign of its approaching death—is already typical of Shakespeare at his mature best. It belongs to the spirit of conscious decline in which the human spirit of the play is now plunged, a decline which Henry's firm affirmation of purpose, though supported by the symbol of justice, cannot altogether conjure: and it leads directly to the return of Pistol, hollow and flamboyant as ever, a singularly appropriate messenger, with his news of the Prince's accession.

On that news, the scene quickly breaks up. Before the "Helicons," the "Africa and golden joys" of Pistol's absurd enthusiasm, the dead become "dunghill curs" to be set aside in the last and most presumptuous adventure of "appetite." The old king, pitifully enough beneath the ridiculous callousness of the phrase, is dead "as nail in door," and in the light of his passing Falstaff, strangely quiet up to this moment, comes to sinister life:

> Away, Bardolph! saddle my horse. Master Robert Shallow, choose what office thou wilt in the land, 'tis thine. . . . I know the young king is sick for me. Let us take any man's horses; the laws of England are at my commandment. Blessed are they that have been my friends; and woe to my lord chief-justice.
>
> (V.iii)

In the light of this, all sentimental approbation of Falstaff is placed finally out of court. This is the voice of "appetite," approaching its prey in the prospect of anarchy: rapacious, cruel—as in Pistol's echoing comment on the Chief-Justice: "Let vultures vile seize on his lungs also!—and blown out, no longer merely with good living,

but with the arrogant self-confidence that anticipates in reality
nothing but its own ruin. The "pleasant days" of Pistol's final dream
will be confronted with reality in the icy wind of righteous authority
that will blow at Westminster; but, inhuman as the wind may seem
and to some extent be, the corruption it blows away will, at least in
the political order, justify it.

One further glimpse of the world of "riot" is afforded us before
the final confrontation of authority and misrule, sober order and
overweening anarchy, takes place. The weight of justice—not the
abstract principle, but its ruthless application—falls first on the
subsidiary creatures of Falstaff's tavern realm, those on whom he has
consistently preyed and who are now swept away into a grim under-
world where feeling, even corrupt and degenerate, can have no place.
The realism is of a kind that will be repeated and extended in later
plays. The writer who conceived the sombre little episode of Doll
Tearsheet's arrest and the cruel clarity of Mistress Quickly's comment, "I pray God the fruit of her womb miscarry," was also the
creator of the low scenes of *Measure for Measure*; in each case, and
allowing for the difference in scale, the intention is intensely serious,
uncompromisingly moral. On each occasion, a fundamental evil, which
in this play Falstaff supremely incarnates, is firmly taken up, delivered
to the "whipping-cheer" which is the real embodiment, at this level,
of the stern proprieties uttered by the Lord Chief-Justice. Its discomfiture, the correction of a state of disease in which physical
reflects moral malady, is necessary, and Henry's own treatment of
Falstaff is about to confirm it; yet even here we are not allowed to
forget that human reactions are at stake, that not all can be gain
in the imposition even of a just order. The final words of Doll and
the Hostess, as they are dragged to correction, stress once more the
wintry conception of justice which prevails throughout:

> *Doll.* Come, you rogue, come; bring me to a justice.
> *Hostess.* Ay, come, you starved blood-hound.
> *Doll.* Goodman death, goodman bones!
> *Hostess.* Thou atomy, thou!

Part of this, necessary and normal as the treatment is by Elizabethan
standards, represents a certain reaction of life against the age, rigidity,
and indifference which have from the first shadowed the operations of
justice in this play; and, in the last resort, the impersonality of the
Beadle's final "Very well" confirms the effect.

These considerations throw light, in turn, upon the famous crux
which rounds off the play—the rejection of Falstaff by the newly
crowned king as he assumes his responsibilities. Falstaff comes to
Westminster full of his new and sinister confidence. He will "leer"

upon the king to attract his favor, he will assume "earnestness of affection," "devotion," associating a feeling which may once have
possessed a certain sincerity with his newly stressed spirit of conscious calculation. The crowning moment is reached when Pistol,
having almost pathetically evoked Doll's imprisonment (almost, because the burlesque intention of his exaltation of her as "Helen of
thy noble thoughts" also belongs to the complete effect), prompts
the pretentious confidence of his reply—"I will deliver her"—and
utters the final phrase "there roar'd the sea, and trumpet-clangor
sounds," in which poetry and base rhetoric are so richly combined.
The moment of settling accounts has at last come and it will show,
among other things, that Doll is far beyond Falstaff's power to
redeem.

The scene, indeed, balances the contrasted themes of the play to
remarkable effect. The breaking of the wave of Falstaff's enthusiasm
against the fixity of the royal purpose is admirably conveyed in
dramatic terms. "God save thy grace, King Hal! my royal Hal!"
Falstaff cries, transported by the prospect of his coming prosperity,
and after Pistol has echoed him—"The heavens thee guard and keep,
most royal imp of fame!"—he further adds, "God save thee, my
sweet boy!" only to find this transport checked by the cold austerity
of Henry's indirect rejoinder: "My lord chief-justice, speak to that
vain man." This in turn leads him to express—this time in terms of
true pathos—his unbelief in what he has heard: "I speak to thee, my
heart," deliberately ignoring the Lord Chief-Justice's reproof: "Have
you your wits? Know you what 'tis you speak?" before he receives
finally, from the king's own mouth, the decisive, unanswerable rejoinder: "I know thee not, old man." The whole exchange is, in its
brevity, marvellously varied, charged with the contrasted motives
that go to make up the play. From this moment, the full content
of the scene is, to a discerning attention, apparent.

Shakespeare, indeed, not only accepted the artistic difficulty involved in the rejection, which the nature of his material and his own
earlier presentation of Falstaff imposed upon him, but wove it into
his own conception; it is a most revealing example of the subjugation
of plot to the growing necessities of expression. For the cleavage
between Falstaff and Hal is a projection of one between unbridled
impulse, which degenerates into swollen disease, and the cold spirit
of successful control, which inevitably becomes inhuman. There is
no doubt that the change noted in the presentation of Falstaff in this
play aims, among other things, at making the rejection at once
feasible and necessary. The Falstaff of Part I would never have allowed himself to be turned off without visible reaction, an aged,
broken shadow, beneath his cynicism, of his former self. It is not

accidental that he has been given a new burden of age, lechery, and disease, which fits in with the changed spirit of the play even as it justifies, and not only in political terms, his treatment at the hands of his former friend. Here, as so often in Shakespeare, we should not simplify the issues. When Henry denounces Falstaff as

> So surfeit-swell'd, so old and so profane,

he is responding to the traditional content of his theme, which called for the young king to reject "riot" on the threshold of his new responsibilities. He makes, in other words, a true criticism which an Elizabethan audience would not have found excessive and which follows inevitably from his changed situation; and the criticism so made is backed with the austerity of a great religious tradition when he adds:

> Make less thy body, hence, and more thy grace.

From the *public* standpoint, which also carries with it in its own sphere a moral implication, this judgement represents a culminating point in the entire action. Henry, as king, cannot but make it, and by making it he lays the foundation of political and moral salvation for his kingdom.

Yet there is, equally, another side to the picture. Though the king's words must be taken at their proper value, the same applies to Falstaff's repeated criticisms of the royal family, which have run as an accompaniment through the preceding action and are no less part of the truth: in much the same way we can accept Isabella's virtue in *Measure for Measure* without closing our eyes to a certain partiality of vision which goes with it. This balancing of the issues, in fact, which should not be confused with indifference and un- willingness to assert judgement, is especially characteristic of the plays of this period. The contrasted characters of Falstaff and Prince Hal, Angelo and Isabella, occupy no more than a part of the whole field of reality which conditions their dramatic being; they are complementary aspects of a creation whose principle of unity lies not solely in the vision of any one of them, but in the author's integration of the various standpoints which constitute his material as a whole. Like Isabella's judgements, though in another degree, those of Henry—valid as they are—suffer from being too easily made. Never is this more so than at this moment, in which he assumes the dignity and impersonality of his vocation. The denial of past friend- ship involved in "I know thee not, old man," the tight-lipped impli- cation of disgust in his advice to "leave gormandizing," the studied gesture to the gallery, so appropriate in one whose life is to be lived from now on as a public function: "Presume not that I am the thing

I was"—all these are as revealing as the afterthought by which
Falstaff, banished scarcely five minutes before, is arrested and thrown
into prison by the returning ministers of the royal justice. This
final severity has been variously interpreted by those who wish it to
fit in with their conception of the new king's character: but surely,
however, we may choose to connect it with Henry's own transformed
nature; its final meaning is related also to the blow that it strikes
at Falstaff's halfhearted attempt to revive his confidence—"I shall be
sent for soon at night"—and with the dissipation of the hopes,
themselves connected with his recent exploitation of Shallow, to
which he clings. This interplay of intimate motives, all relevant and
none final, we should by now have learnt to see as a characteristic
manifestation of Shakespeare's genius.

The final condemnation of Falstaff is accompanied, typically, by
Lancaster's flat and unpleasing comment:

> I like this fair proceeding of the king's:
> He hath intent his wonted followers
> Shall all be very well provided for.

The concluding provision for Falstaff, though it clearly corresponds
to an effort to justify the royal action in public terms, is only on the
public plane satisfactory:

> For competence of life I will allow you,
> That lack of means enforce you not to evil:
> And, as we hear you do reform yourselves,
> We will, according to your strengths and qualities,
> Give you advancement.
>
> (V.v)

Though perhaps a sufficient justification of the king, it does not
help us to form a kinder estimate of the man. The comment surely
needs to be read in the light of Falstaff's death as announced in
Henry V. Far from being an afterthought, or—as some have held—a
practical device to dispose of a character whom Shakespeare himself,
having created him, could neither repeat indefinitely nor allow to
dominate his political conception, Falstaff's death is surely the logical
conclusion of this action and has been prepared for by the change in
sentiment that has been increasingly evident in *Henry IV, Part II*.
Death and mortality are of the essence of this play, and if the
political development is dominated by these realities, so that only
the rigid imposition of the will to govern, exercised in the common
good, can obtain some measure of triumph over it, it is logical that
the humanity which that will cannot compass, having undergone a
corruption of its own, should finally die. Fair provision by the grace

of the new order is no destiny for the creature that Falstaff has been. Even in his old age, his spirit is nearer to the related decay and tenderness of the exchange with Doll Tearsheet: and since neither tenderness nor decay has henceforth any real part in the new king's character, his death, and not merely his exposure as a symbol of "riot," is inevitable.

There is no need, in the last analysis, to be sentimental on behalf of either the Prince or Falstaff. The "unpleasantness" in their relationship is a necessary part of the play. It springs from all that is most individual in its conception; it translates yet again into dramatic terms of personal opposition the "disease" which we have found hanging over the English state, and it relates all the division between age and youth, action and inaction, anarchic folly and cold calculation which embody that disease to a developing split in the dramatist's conception of the world as his plays reveal it. The precise meaning, in terms of the sensibility here revealed, of this bitter contrast between aged dissolution and the controlled frigidity so unnaturally ascribed to youth, needs to be defined in relation to certain of the Sonnets, to *Troilus and Cressida,* and to *Measure for Measure. Henry IV, Part II,* provides, in a word, through the presentation of a society in which the normal attributes of life are subject to a peculiar and disquieting inversion, a fruitful approach to the issues more completely handled by Shakespeare in the first plays of his maturity.

PART TWO

View Points

A. C. Bradley: The Rejection of Falstaff

To come, then, to Henry. Both as prince and as king he is deservedly a favourite, and particularly so with English readers, being, as he is, perhaps the most distinctively English of all Shakespeare's men. In *Henry V* he is treated as a national hero. In this play he has lost much of the wit which in him seems to have depended on contact with Falstaff, but he has also laid aside the most serious faults of his youth. He inspires in a high degree fear, enthusiasm, and affection; thanks to his beautiful modesty he has the charm which is lacking to another mighty warrior, Coriolanus; his youthful escapades have given him an understanding of simple folk, and sympathy with them; he is the author of the saying, "There is some soul of goodness in things evil"; and he is much more obviously religious than most of Shakespeare's heroes. Having these and other fine qualities, and being without certain dangerous tendencies which mark the tragic heroes, he is, perhaps, the most *efficient* character drawn by Shakespeare, unless Ulysses, in *Troilus and Cressida,* is his equal. And so he has been described as Shakespeare's ideal man of action; nay, it has even been declared that here for once Shakespeare plainly disclosed his own ethical creed, and showed us his ideal, not simply of a man of action, but of a man.

But Henry is neither of these. The poet who drew Hamlet and Othello can never have thought that even the ideal man of action would lack that light upon the brow which at once transfigures them and marks their doom. It is as easy to believe that, because the lunatic, the lover, and the poet are not far apart, Shakespeare would have chosen never to have loved and sung. Even poor Timon, the most inefficient of the tragic heroes, has something in him that Henry never shows. Nor is it merely that his nature is limited: if we follow Shakespeare and look closely at Henry, we shall discover with the many fine traits a few less pleasing. Henry IV describes him as the noble image of his own youth; and, for all his superiority to his father, he is still his father's son, the son of the man whom Hotspur called a "vile

From "The Rejection of Falstaff," in Oxford Lectures on Poetry (London: Macmillan & Co., Ltd., 1959), pp. 256–60. Reprinted by permission of St. Martin's Press, Inc., The Macmillan Company of Canada, Ltd., and Macmillan & Co., Ltd.

politician." Henry's religion, for example, is genuine, it is rooted in
his modesty; but it is also superstitious—an attempt to buy off super-
natural vengeance for Richard's blood; and it is also in part political,
like his father's projected crusade. Just as he went to war chiefly because, as his father told him, it was the way to keep factious nobles
quiet and unite the nation, so when he adjures the Archbishop to
satisfy him as to his right to the French throne, he knows very well
that the Archbishop *wants* the war, because it will defer and perhaps
prevent what he considers the spoliation of the Church. This same
strain of policy is what Shakespeare marks in the first soliloquy in
Henry IV, where the prince describes his riotous life as a mere scheme
to win him glory later. It implies that readiness to use other people
as means to his own ends which is a conspicuous feature in his father;
and it reminds us of his father's plan of keeping himself out of the
people's sight while Richard was making himself cheap by his inces-
sant public appearances. And if I am not mistaken there is a further
likeness. Henry is kindly and pleasant to every one as Prince, to every
one deserving as King; and he is so not merely out of policy: but
there is no sign in him of a strong affection for any one, such an affection as we recognise at a glance in Hamlet and Horatio, Brutus and
Cassius, and many more. We do not find this in *Henry V,* not even in
the noble address to Lord Scroop, and in *Henry IV* we find, I think,
a liking for Falstaff and Poins, but no more: there is no more than a
liking, for instance, in his soliloquy over the supposed corpse of his
fat friend, and he never speaks of Falstaff to Poins with any affection.
The truth is, that the members of the family of Henry IV have love
for one another, but they cannot spare love for any one outside their
family, which stands firmly united, defending its royal position against
attack and instinctively isolating itself from outside influence.

Thus I would suggest that Henry's conduct in his rejection of Falstaff is in perfect keeping with his character on its unpleasant side as
well as on its finer; and that, so far as Henry is concerned, we ought
not to feel surprise at it. And on this view we may even explain the
strange incident of the Chief Justice being sent back to order Falstaff
to prison (for there is no sign of any such uncertainty in the text as
might suggest an interpolation by the players). Remembering his
father's words about Henry, "Being incensed, he's flint," and remembering in *Henry V* his ruthlessness about killing the prisoners when
he is incensed, we may imagine that, after he had left Falstaff and was
no longer influenced by the face of his old companion, he gave way
to anger at the indecent familiarity which had provoked a compromising scene on the most ceremonial of occasions and in the presence
alike of court and crowd, and that he sent the Chief Justice back to
take vengeance. And this is consistent with the fact that in the next

play we find Falstaff shortly afterwards not only freed from prison, but unmolested in his old haunt in Eastcheap, well within ten miles of Henry's person. His anger had soon passed, and he knew that the requisite effect had been produced both on Falstaff and on the world. But all this, however true, will not solve our problem. It seems, on the contrary, to increase its difficulty. For the natural conclusion is that Shakespeare *intended* us to feel resentment against Henry. And yet that cannot be, for it implies that he meant the play to end disagreeably; and no one who understands Shakespeare at all will consider that supposition for a moment credible. No; he must have meant the play to end pleasantly, although he made Henry's action consistent. And hence it follows that he must have intended our sympathy with Falstaff to be so far weakened when the rejection-scene arrives that his discomfiture should be satisfactory to us; that we should enjoy this sudden reverse of enormous hopes (a thing always ludicrous if sympathy is absent); that we should approve the moral judgment that falls on him; and so should pass lightly over that disclosure of unpleasant traits in the King's character which Shakespeare was too true an artist to suppress. Thus our pain and resentment, if we feel them, are wrong, in the sense that they do not answer to the dramatist's intention. But it does not follow that they are wrong in a further sense. They may be right, because the dramatist has missed what he aimed at. And this, though the dramatist was Shakespeare, is what I would suggest. In the Falstaff scenes he overshot his mark. He created so extraordinary a being, and fixed him so firmly on his intellectual throne, that when he sought to dethrone him he could not. The moment comes when we are to look at Falstaff in a serious light, and the comic hero is to figure as a baffled schemer; but we cannot make the required change, either in our attitude or in our sympathies. We wish Henry a glorious reign and much joy of his crew of hypocritical politicians, lay and clerical; but our hearts go with Falstaff to the Fleet, or, if necessary, to Arthur's bosom or wheresomever he is.[1]

J. Dover Wilson: King Henry's Speech

If my readers have followed me to this point they will, I think, be prepared to agree that the rejection has become inevitable. Ought

From "King Henry's Speech," in The Fortunes of Falstaff (New York and London: Cambridge University Press, 1943), pp. 120–23. Reprinted by permission of the author and publisher.

[1] That from the beginning Shakespeare intended Henry's accession to be Fal-

we, nevertheless, to resent with Bradley the manner in which it is
carried out? My reply is that what he calls the "sermon" [1] is in keeping at once with Hal's character and with his situation, and not only
dramatically effective but probably the only effective way of termi-
nating the play which Shakespeare could have devised. Let readers
and spectators put themselves first in the young King's place, and
then in his creator's, and ask themselves what else either could have
done in the circumstances. Having watched him kneeling at his
father's death-bed and heard him making his noble peace with the
Lord Chief Justice, we can be certain, and should be fully aware,
that at this moment, with the crown of England newly placed upon
his head, the chrism still glistening upon his forehead, and his spirit
uplifted by one of the most solemn acts of dedication and consecration which the Christian Church has to offer, all his thoughts and
emotions will be concentrated upon the great task to which he has
been called, its duties and responsibilities. It is a fatal moment for
Falstaff to present himself. Even Bradley admits that the rogue now
behaves "in so fatuous and outrageous a manner that great sternness
on the King's part was unavoidable." [2] May we not go farther and
say that anger would be both natural and excusable to anyone in
such a mood, more especially to one who, "being incensed," is "flint"?

The job had to be done, a clean cut made; and on every count it
had to be made publicly. Bradley contradicts himself, in effect, by
suggesting on the one hand that Hal should have communicated his
decision to Falstaff "in a private interview rich in humour and merely
touched with pathos," and, by complaining on the other hand, that
"Shakespeare has so contrived matters" that no such "private warning" is possible.[3] The truth is surely that Shakespeare very well knew
that any talk of a private nature between Hal and Falstaff at this
juncture would be too difficult even for his powers. It is not that
Harry, as some would hold, would find the double pull of old affections and improvised brilliance, as always, quite irresistible, but that
Shakespeare himself has been busy ever since Shrewsbury manoeu-
vring these former friends into different universes between which
conversation is impossible. And if the language of the speech sounds
formal and homiletic, that is because Hal is learning to speak, not

---

staff's catastrophe is clear from the fact that, when the two characters first appear,
Falstaff is made to betray at once the hopes with which he looks forward to Henry's
reign. See the First Part of *Henry IV*, Act I, Scene ii.
  [1] *Oxford Lectures*, p. 253.
  [2] *Ibid.*, p. 253.
  [3] *Oxford Lectures*, p. 253.

as Bradley complains "like a clergyman," [4] but like the Chief Justice, to whom he had just promised that his voice should sound as he did prompt his ear. The adoption of the Justice as his father and the consecration at the Abbey had completed the process of separation, and the only speech the regenerate Harry can now have with his old Adam is a public one.

Not that he relishes the task or finds it easy. When Falstaff first confronts him, and that great red face breaks in upon his "white celestial thought," he tries to avoid the encounter, begging the Lord Chief Justice to say for him what must be said. But Falstaff, on fire with anticipation, brushes the old judge aside, so that there is nothing for it: the King must speak the unpleasant words himself. And just because they have to be unpleasant, unpleasant to himself as well as to the man he addresses, to say nothing of the publicity and the fact that his brothers, the court and the Chief Justice stand there listening how he will comport himself after his recent announcement of reformation, will he not be on his mettle and perhaps use language blunter and harsher than he might otherwise have done? Even so, he falters and finds it difficult to keep it up. For, as Warburton has shrewdly observed, having used the word "gormandizing" by chance, and

that word unluckily presenting him with a pleasant idea, he cannot forbear pursuing it—

> Know the grave doth gape
> For thee thrice wider than for other men—

and is just falling back into Hal, by a humorous allusion to Falstaff's bulk; but he perceives it immediately, and fearing Sir John should take the advantage of it, checks both himself and the knight, with—

> Reply not to me with a fool-born jest;

and so resumes the thread of his discourse.[5]

As for

> I know thee not, old man. Fall to thy prayers,

and the rest of it, while such sentiments may be harsh, to call them "ungenerous" is to misapprehend the relationship between the knight and his patron, and to call them "dishonest" is even more absurd. The terms are again Bradley's, who goes so far as to stigmatize the speech as "an attempt to buy the praise of the respectable at the cost

[4] *Ibid.*, p. 254.
[5] *V.* Johnson's *Shakespeare*, iv, pp. 352–3.

of honour and truth." [6] Charges of this kind would never, I think, have occurred to a critic before the end of the nineteenth century. Respectability, the word and the social quality, were of mid-eighteenth century origin, and did not even begin to fall into disfavour until at least a hundred years later; about which time the phenomenon of conversion, of which the change in Henry Monmouth is an example, also ceased to be regarded as normal or desirable by average serious-minded persons. King Henry V is a new man; he had buried his "wildness' in his father's grave; he speaks as the representative and embodiment of

> The majesty and power of law and justice.[7]

I cannot believe that members of an Elizabethan audience would have felt the "sermon" anything but fine and appropriate. And if some, as Rowe suggests, may have "in remembrance of the diversion" Falstaff "had formerly afforded 'em, been sorry to see his friend Hal use him so scurvily," [8] others would assuredly have retorted with Johnson:

> but if it be considered that the fat knight has never uttered one senti-
> ment of generosity, and with all his power of exciting mirth, has nothing
> in him that can be esteemed, no great pain will be suffered from the
> reflection that he is compelled to live honestly, and maintained by
> the King, with a promise of advancement when he shall deserve it.[9]

As for ourselves, how characteristically muddleheaded it is that a generation which has almost universally condemned a prince of its own for putting private inclinations before his public obligations, should condemn Hal as a cad and a prig for doing just the opposite.

But more important than all these questions of moral decorum, which are the plague of modern dramatic criticism, are those of dramatic decorum, in which critics of a former age took greater interest. And here, at any rate, there can be no question of the rightness of Shakespeare's finale. Preparing his audience for the rejection from the beginning, and making it appear ever more inevitable the nearer he approaches to it, in the end he springs it upon them in the most striking and unexpected fashion possible. Under the conditions of stage-performance, the only conditions which Shakespeare contemplated, both the encounter outside the Abbey and the speech of the King are extraordinarily effective.

[6] *Oxford Lectures,* p. 254.
[7] Pt. II, 5. 2. 78.
[8] Ed. 1709, p. xviii.
[9] Johnson, *op. cit.,* iv, p. 353.

E. M. W. Tillyard: From Shakespeare's History Plays

The structure of the two parts is indeed very similar. In the first part the Prince (who, one knows, will soon be king) is tested in the military or chivalric virtues. He has to choose, Morality-fashion, between Sloth or Vanity, to which he is drawn by his bad companions, and Chivalry, to which he is drawn by his father and his brothers. And he chooses Chivalry. The action is complicated by Hotspur and Falstaff, who stand for the excess and the defect of the military spirit, for honour exaggerated and dishonour. Thus the Prince, as well as being Magnificence in a Morality Play, is Aristotle's middle quality between two extremes. Such a combination would have been entirely natural to the Elizabethans, especially since it occurred in the second book of the *Fairy Queen*. Guyon is at once the Morality figure fought over by the Palmer and Mammon and the man who is shown the Aristotelian allegory of Excess Balance and Defect in Perissa Medina and Elissa. Near the end of the play the Prince ironically surrenders to Falstaff the credit of having killed Hotspur, thus leaving the world of arms and preparing for the motive of the second part. Here again he is tested, but in the civil virtues. He has to choose, Morality-fashion, between disorder or misrule, to which he is drawn by his bad companions, and Order or Justice (the supreme kingly virtue) to which he is drawn by his father and by his father's deputy the Lord Chief Justice. And he chooses Justice. As in the first part the Aristotelian motive occurs, but it is only touched on. After Falstaff has exchanged words with John of Lancaster about his captive Sir John Colevile, he remains on the stage to soliloquize. He calls John a "sober-blooded boy" and blames him for not drinking sack. John is thus cold-blooded and addicted to thin potations; Falstaff himself is warm-blooded and addicted to strong drink. The Prince is the mean, cold-blooded by inheritance but warmed "with excellent endeavour of drinking good and good store of fertile sherris." Temperamentally he strikes the balance between the parsimony of John and the extravagance of Falstaff. He does the same too in his practice of justice. The justice of John of Lancaster in his cold-blooded treatment of

From Shakespeare's History Plays (*New York: The Macmillan Company, 1946; London: Chatto & Windus, Ltd., 1946), pp. 265, 66. Copyright © 1946 by The Macmillan Company. Reprinted by permission of Stephen Tillyard and the publishers.*

the rebels verges on rigour; Falstaff has no general standard of justice at all; Henry V uses his justice moderately in the way he treats his old companions—at least by Elizabethan standards. . . .

In the second part the military theme of the rebellion is continued, but the Prince resigns his share in it to his brother John. He has proved his worth in chivalry; he must now prove it in civil life. As in the first part he begins with appearances against him. He has indulged his inclination to vanity by providing Falstaff with a page, and he has applied military methods to civil life (as well as indulging his passions) by striking the Lord Chief Justice. But we learn this by hearsay only: as he draws nearer to the throne the Prince must be less openly given to mischief. In compensation, the opposing principles between which he has to choose are brought face to face, as they never were in the first part. Thus there are two scenes of sparring between Falstaff and the Lord Chief Justice. During the first of these we learn that the Justice has scored a point by having advised the king to post Falstaff to John of Lancaster's army, thus separating him from the Prince. In the middle portion of the play the Morality theme is kept in suspense, while other important business is transacted. The action broadens to include many phases of English life; Falstaff indulges in adventures that have nothing to do with the Prince; the political theme of Henry IV's many troubles draws to a close. Shakespeare naturally reassures us that the main action is only in suspense: for instance in the tavern scene with Falstaff and Doll Tearsheet the Prince recollects his duties when Peto enters with the news that the king is back at Westminster awaiting news of the Yorkshire rebels. The crisis comes just before the king's death, when the Prince persuades his father that he took the crown from his father's bedside in error, not out of indecent haste to begin a riotous reign. *We* are persuaded too and know that he will accept the rule of the Lord Chief Justice, who committed him to prison, and reject his old companions. Shakespeare knits the end closely not only to the beginning of Part Two but to the whole play. For instance, Falstaff recalls his opposition to his chief enemy and hence the Morality pattern by his last words as he leaves Gloucestershire to salute the new king: "Woe to my Lord Chief Justice." But it is Henry V's words, as he rejects Falstaff, that have the function of gathering the themes together. Henry does not merely preach at Falstaff: every unkind thing he says and every piece of moral advice he gives echo words spoken to or by Falstaff. "Fall to thy prayers" says Henry; and we should think of his earlier words to Falstaff: "I see a good amendment of life in thee, from praying to purse-taking" spoken in the second scene of Part One, and "Say thy prayers and farewell" spoken in a very different tone before the Battle of Shrewsbury. When Henry says

How ill white hairs become a fool and jester,

we should remember (as Falstaff must have remembered) the Chief Justice's words, "There is not a white hair on your face but should have his effect of gravity." And when Henry speaks of the grave gaping for him, we should remember Doll's remark to Falstaff about "patching up thine old body for heaven" and Falstaff's reply of "Peace, good Doll! do not speak like a death's-head; do not bid me remember mine end." These echoes do not make Henry V's speech any kinder but they give it a great deal of point.

Harold Jenkins: From The Structural Problem in Shakespeare's Henry the Fourth

Part 2 itself does not require extended treatment. For whenever it was "planned," it is a consequence of Part 1. Its freedom is limited by the need to present what Part 1 so plainly prepared for and then left out. Falstaff cannot be allowed to escape a second time. His opposition to the law, being now the dominant interest, accordingly shapes the plot; and the law, now bodied forth in the half-legendary figure of the Lord Chief Justice, becomes a formidable person in the drama. The opening encounter between these two, in which Falstaff makes believe not to see or hear his reprover, is symbolic of Falstaff's whole attitude to law—he ignores its existence as long as he can. But the voice which he at first refuses to hear is the voice which will pronounce his final sentence. The theme of the individual versus the law proves so fertile that it readily gives rise to subplots. Justice Shallow, of course, claims his place in the play by virtue of the life that is in him, exuberant in the capers of senility itself. He functions all the same as the Lord Chief Justice's antithesis: he is the foolish justice with whom Falstaff has his way and from whom he wrings the thousand pounds that the wise justice has denied him. Even Shallow's servant Davy has his relation to the law; and his view of law is that though a man may be a knave, if he is my friend and I am the justice's servant, it is hard if the knave cannot win. In this humane sentiment Davy takes on full vitality as a person; but he simultaneously brings us back to confront at a different angle the main moral issue of the play. Is he to control the law or the law him? In fact, shall Falstaff flourish or shall a thief be hanged?

It has sometimes been objected that Falstaff runs away with Part

From The Structural Problem in Shakespeare's *Henry the Fourth (London: Methuen & Co., Ltd., 1956), pp. 23–27. Copyright © Methuen & Co., Ltd. Reprinted by permission of the publisher.*

2. In truth he has to shoulder the burden of it because a dead man and a converted one can give him small assistance. Part 2 has less opportunity for the integrated double action of Part 1. To be sure, it attempts a double action, and has often been observed to be in some respects a close replica of Part 1—"almost a carbon copy," Professor Shaaber says. At exactly the same point in each part, for example, is a little domestic scene where a rebel leader contemplates leaving home, and in each part this is directly followed by the big tavern scene in which revelry rises to a climax. And so on. An article in a recent number of *The Review of English Studies* has even called *Henry IV* a diptych, finding the "parallel presentation of incidents" in the two parts the primary formal feature. I do not wish to deny the aesthetic satisfaction to be got from a recognition of this rhythmic repetition; yet it is only the more superficial pattern that can be thus repeated. With history and Holinshed obliging, rebellion can break out as before; yet the rebellion of Part 2, though it occupies our attention, has no significance, nor can have, for the principal characters of the play. The story of the Prince and Hotspur is over, and the King has only to die.

The one thing about history is that it does not repeat itself. Hotspur, unlike Sherlock Holmes, cannot come back to life. But there are degrees in all things; conversion has not quite the same finality as death. And besides, there is a type of hero whose adventures always can recur. Robin Hood has no sooner plundered one rich man than another comes along. It is the nature of Brer Fox, and indeed of Dr. Watson, to be incapable of learning from experience. In folk-lore, that is to say, though not in history, you can be at the same point twice. And it seems as if Prince Hal may be sufficient of a folk-lore hero to be permitted to go again through the cycle of riot and reform. In Part 2 as in Part 1 the King laments his son's unprincely life. Yet this folk-lore hero is also a historical, and what is more to the point, a dramatic personage, and it is not tolerable that the victor of Shrewsbury should do as critics sometimes say he does, relapse into his former wildness and then reform again. The Prince cannot come into Part 2 unreclaimed without destroying the dramatic effect of Part 1. Yet if Part 2 is not to forgo its own dramatic effect, and especially its splendid last-act peripeteia, it requires a prince who is unreclaimed. This is Part 2's dilemma, and the way that it takes out of it is a bold one. When the King on his deathbed exclaims against the Prince's "headstrong riot," he has not forgotten that at Shrewsbury he congratulated the Prince on his redemption. He has not forgotten it for the simple reason that it has never taken place. The only man at court who believes in the Prince's reformation, the Earl of Warwick, believes that it will happen, not that it has happened already. Even as we watch the hero repeating his folklore cycle, we are positively instructed that he has not been here before:

> The tide of blood in me
> Hath proudly flow'd in vanity till now.

In the two parts of *Henry IV* there are not two princely reformations but two versions of a single reformation. And they are mutually exclusive.[1] Though Part 2 frequently recalls and sometimes depends on what has happened in Part 1, it also denies that Part 1 exists. Accordingly the ideal spectator of either part must not cry with Shakespeare's Lucio, "I know what I know." He must sometimes remember what he knows and sometimes be content to forget it. This, however, is a requirement made in some degree by any work of fiction, or as they used to call it, feigning. And the feat is not a difficult one for those accustomed to grant the poet's demand for "that willing suspension of disbelief . . . which constitutes poetic faith."

Henry IV, then, is both one play and two. Part 1 begins an action which it finds it has not scope for but which Part 2 rounds off. But with one half of the action already concluded in Part 1, there is danger of a gap in Part 2. To stop the gap Part 2 expands the unfinished story of Falstaff and reduplicates what is already finished in the story of the Prince. The two parts are complementary, they are also independent and even incompatible. What they are, with their various formal anomalies, I suppose them to have become through what Johnson termed "the necessity of exhibition." Though it would be dangerous to dispute Coleridge's view that a work of art must "contain in itself the reason why it is so," that its form must proceed from within,[2] yet even works of art, like other of man's productions, must submit to the bondage of the finite. Even the unwieldy novels of the Victorians, as recent criticism has been showing, obey the demands of their allotted three volumes of space; and the dramatic masterpieces of any age, no less than inaugural lectures, must acknowledge the dimensions of time.

[1] All this is very well exhibited by H. E. Cain ("Further Light on the Relation of *1* and *2 Henry IV*," *Shakespeare Quarterly*, III (1952), 21 ff.). But his conclusion that the two parts therefore have no continuity is invalidated because, like many others, he is content to isolate particular elements in the problem and does not examine it whole. Except when the views of others are being quoted or discussed, the word "Falstaff" does not occur in his article.

[2] This is a synthesis of several passages in Coleridge. The words in quotation marks are said of whatever can give permanent pleasure; but the context shows Coleridge to be thinking of literary composition. See *Biographia Literaria*, ed. Shawcross, ii. 9. Also relevant are "On Poesy or Art," *ibid.*, ii. 262; and *Coleridge's Shakespearean Criticism*, ed. T. M. Raysor, i. 223–4.

A. P. *Rossiter:* Ambivalence: The Dialectic of the Histories

Throughout the Histories it is in the implications of the Comic that shrewd, realistic thinking about men in politics—in office—in war—in plot—is exposed: realistic apprehension outrunning the medieval frame. Because the Tudor myth system of Order, Degree, etc. was too rigid, too black-and-white, too doctrinaire and narrowly moral for Shakespeare's mind: it falsified his fuller experience of men. Consequently, while employing it as *frame,* he had to undermine it, to qualify it with equivocations: to vex its applications with sly or subtle ambiguities: to cast doubt on its ultimate human validity, even in situations where its principles seemed most completely applicable. His intuition told him it was *morally* inadequate.

Hence the unhappy feelings which generous-minded critics have displayed about the Rejection of Falstaff. That some of them have *overdone* it is neither here nor there. It is well enough for Dr. Tillyard or Professor Dover Wilson to tell us that the Prince *had* to cast off Sir John. We know that. We know what Kingship meant to textbook Tudors (far better than the Globe audiences knew, I dare say). Yet I still feel that as Shakespeare *was* Shakespeare—the man who made Hermione and Hamlet, drew Kate Percy as war-widow (a traitor's wife by the Code), drew Katherine as the fallen majesty of England—he must have known, *and felt,* the lack of humanity (of generosity, high-mindedness, true magnanimity) in his Hal in that scene. And again, I think, in Henry's treatment of the conspirators at Southampton; where the king is so obviously playing a publicity propaganda part, as Justice, iron-visaged, pitiless. . . . As obviously as he said he was in that first of unprincely soliloquies, "I know you all. . . ." (*1 Henry IV,* I.ii.end.).

Is there not a resemblant quality in his father: the "silent king," Bolingbroke, in the mirror-episode in *Richard II?* A separateness from the feeling world, which makes the actor in public affairs assume a predetermined part, like a *play*-actor, only with all his directives outside and none of his? One of those "who, moving others, are themselves as stone," as the sonnet phrases it: "the lords and owners of

From *"Ambivalence: The Dialectic of the Histories,"* in Angel with Horns, ed. *Graham Storey (London: Longmans, Green & Co., Ltd., 1961), pp. 59–61. Reprinted by permission of Hodder & Stoughton, Ltd. and Max Reinhardt, Ltd., London, and Theatre Arts Books, New York. Originally published in* Talking of Shakespeare, *ed. John Garrett (London: Hodder & Stoughton, Ltd. and Max Reinhardt, Ltd., 1954).*

their faces"? And thus again a resemblant quality in John of Lancaster's treachery to the northern rebels? Oh, I know it can be argued that, to the Elizabethans, no ill treatment or trickery towards rebels could be unjustified. But can we assume that Shakespeare's sensibilities were so crass as not to know meanness as meanness, perfidy as perfidy, when it could be said to have profited the State? I say no more than, "I think not." And if you agree on any of these points I've hung on to the Rejection of Falstaff, doesn't it follow that you are made to *feel* (not merely "see," notionally) how the frame of Order, the coherent rigid medieval system accepted by some of our most reputed modern scholars, is outrun by that mind which Jonson (who "knew the man. . . . etc.") considered to be "not for an age but for all time"?

It follows, if I have taken you along with me, that we cannot dissect-out, stain and fix the system of Shakespeare's reflexion on History. A rigid political-moral good-and-evil system is there; but as the events and the people speak into our inner mind, we find that Shakespeare is shifting subtly from key to key, as if by what musicians call "enharmonic changes": using ambiguous note-sequences till contradiction is itself confounded, and yields a precise evocation of the paradox of human experience.

R. J. Dorius: A Little More than a Little

When Henry V banishes the "tutor and the feeder of my riots" at the end of Part II, he speaks of his companionship with Falstaff as a "dream," which—"being awak'd" and watching for sleeping England—he now despises (II:V.v.53–55). The younger Henry apparently dreams of Falstaff as Richard II seemed to dream of Bolingbroke in England's garden, but unlike Richard, he does not succumb to his nightmare. Some critics have been offended by an image (among others) from Henry's rejection speech which the metaphors we have been following should help to deepen and justify:[1] "Make less thy body, hence, and more thy grace;/Leave gormandizing" (56–57). To throw these words and this controversial scene into larger perspective, we must give appropriate emphasis to the virtues of law and order em-

---

From "A Little More than a Little," in Shakespeare Quarterly, XI (1960), 13–26. Copyright © 1960 by the Shakespeare Association of America, Inc. Reprinted by permission of the author and publisher.

[1] The author has been discussing the way in which the cardinal virtues of the histories—prudence, economy, and strength of character (kingliness)—are explored in the second tetralogy through images which illustrate the extremes—waste and destruction, fatness or excessive growth—"of which economy is the mean or the ends to which extravagance in man or government might lead." [Editor's Note.]

bodied in the Chief Justice and of prudence and economy running through all of the histories. And we must remember the surprising seriousness with which Falstaff defends himself and the Prince promises to banish him ("I do, I will") during the mock interview—really the trial of a way of life—in Part I (II:iv.462–528). Both seem to know from the beginning that this dream will end. But the complexity of Falstaff and of our attitudes toward him is the best measure of the delicate balance among political and moral attitudes maintained throughout these plays.

The sympathy of the world has always been with the fat knight, and the popularity of these plays would be vastly reduced if, unimaginably, he were not in them. The Prince's turning from "plump Jack," "All the world," can be seen as the rejection of fuller life in favor of power, of being for becoming. That Jack is perhaps an inevitable companion for the Prince, Henry IV makes plain when he associates fatness with nobility in speaking of his son: "Most subject is the fattest soil to weeds;/And he, the noble image of my youth,/Is overspread with them" (II:IV.iv.54–56). But in a comic but highly significant defense of the medicine he recommends for every illness, Falstaff says that the royal blood or soil in Hal was originally "lean, sterile, and bare" and had to be "manured, husbanded, and till'd" with "fertile sherris" to make Hal "valiant" (II:IV.iii.92–135). Falstaff's phenomenal attractiveness and his mockery of honor and all state affairs give us, among other things, just the insight we need into the "cold blood" of the Lancasters, and also into the dying chivalric code for which his "catechism" (I:V.i.128–140) is a kind of epitaph or *reductio ad absurdum*. But the parallels between the sustained imagery we have been following and Shakespeare's characterization of Falstaff emphasize a darker side of this hill of flesh and illuminate his profoundly functional role in this entire cycle of plays.

Far from threatening the structure of the histories, as some have maintained, Falstaff is one of their central organizing symbols. It is tempting to guess that Shakespeare rapidly found the imagery drawn from nature and animal life which is so marked a feature of the style of *Henry VI* and, far more subtly and intricately, of *Richard II*, inadequate for his increasingly complicated meanings. However we account for it, he developed or chanced upon another and far more expressive vehicle for the ideas of the sick state and king associated in *Richard II* with the overgrown garden. The final evolution of the metaphor of the fat garden and of the sick body politic is probably the fat man. Metaphors from the unweeded garden may underline or even symbolize the sickness of the realm, to be sure, but the tun of man can also, if as alert and witty as Falstaff, make the best possible case for fatness, for the "sin" of being "old and merry," for "instinct" and life rather than grinning honor and death. And he can afford us the point of view from which thinness and economy can be seen as inadequate or unpleasant characteristics. Thus he can throw into clearer relief the entire political and personal ethic of the histories. If we compare the relatively simple equivalence between the physical ugliness of the "elvishmark'd, abortive, rooting hog," Richard III, and the disordered state, on the one hand, with the ambivalent richness of the relationships between the "shapes" of Falstaff and rebellious England, on the other, we can have a helpful index of the deepening of Shakespeare's thought and his growing mastery of his medium over the five or six years (1592–3 to 1597–8) that separate the first of the major histories from the greatest.

Falstaff, then, is both the sickness of the state, the prince of the caterpillars preying on the commonwealth, and the remedy for some of its ills. And his role dramatizes the gulf between the essential virtues of the private man and those of the ruler, for as we see in *Antony,* the feast which nourishes the one sickens the other. Timeless Falstaff is in a curiously reciprocal relationship with time-serving Henry IV, for they are the principal competitors for the Prince's allegiance, in affording by precept and example radically contrasting mirrors for the young magistrate. But the usurper who disdained to follow the example of rioting Richard, as we have seen, finds his eldest son rioting with Falstaff—a kind of embodiment of Henry's inability to weed his own garden. Both the politician and the reveler must disappear from the world of young Henry V before he can find his own voice somewhere between them. He had to befriend Falstaff to know this man's gifts and "language," and in the "perfectness of time" he had to act to arrest the threat of such "gross terms" to the kingdom (II:IV. iv.68–75). The threat is real, for Falstaff is almost the result of a process similar to that referred to by the Archbishop in defending the rebels in Part II: "The time misord'red doth, in common sense,/Crowd us and crush us to this monstrous form . . ." (II:IV.ii.33–34). We can hardly sentimentalize a Falstaff who says he will "turn diseases to commodity" (II:I.ii.277), when we remember the Bastard's great attack upon "commodity" (opportunism, time-serving) in the nearly contemporary *King John.*[2] And we cannot ignore the outrageousness of Falstaff's cry upon hearing of Hal's succession, just before he himself is banished: "Let us take any man's horses; the laws of England are at

---

[2] As has frequently been observed, the Falstaff of Part II is a less complicated and attractive figure than the Falstaff of Part I. Increasingly obsessed with his age, his aches and diseases, and, being rarely in the company of the Prince, at once more arrogant and less witty, he seems to embody less of the high-spiritedness which the Lancastrians lack and more of the corruption which threatens to engulf the kingdom.

my commandment" (II:V.iii.141–142). Falstaff threatens to usurp the "customary rights" of time, governed as he says he is only by the moon, and to make the law "bondslave" to lawlessness.

Falstaff is depicted in language very similar to that employed in two of the most vivid pictures of disorder in all of Shakespeare, both of them from *2 Henry IV*. Once in a kind of mock despair, the wily Northumberland prays that "order die!/And let this world no longer be a stage/To feed contention in a ling'ring act . . ." (I.i.154–156). Later, the dying king, apprehensive lest his realm receive the "scum" of "neighbour confines" and become a "wilderness," fears that Hal will

> Pluck down my officers, break my decrees;
> For now a time is come to mock at form.
> Harry the Fifth is crown'd. Up, vanity . . .
> For the Fifth Harry from curb'd license plucks
> The muzzle of restraint, and the wild dog
> Shall flesh his tooth on every innocent.
>   (IV.v.118–20,131–33)

The formless man, "vanity in years," who has mocked at all forms of honor has been the prince's closest companion, potentially a powerful voice in state affairs. The real target of the "fool and jest" has been the "rusty curb of old father antic the law" (I:I.ii.69–70), and the violence in the lines above of "wild dog" and "flesh" reminds us of the "butcher" of the histories, Richard III, and of the cormorant-villains of the tragedies. The rejection of Falstaff marks the new king's turning from the negligence and excess that had nearly destroyed England since the reign of Richard II. As the young king dismisses one tutor and embraces another in the Chief Justice, he cultivates his garden in "law and form and due proportion":

> The tide of blood in me
> Hath proudly flow'd in vanity till now.
> Now doth it turn and ebb back to the sea,
> Where it shall mingle with the state of floods
> And flow henceforth in formal majesty.
>   (II:V.ii:129–133)

The proud river of the private will has become the sea of life of the commonwealth. The blood which here as in the tragedies is the basis of both mood and mind is purged. The man who said he was of all humors comes to achieve the "finely bolted" balance which Henry once thought characterized the traitor Scroop:

> spare in diet,
> Free from gross passion or of mirth or anger . . .

Not working with the eye without the ear,
And but in purged judgment trusting neither.
(*H.V.*,II.ii.131–136)

Henry V is by no means the kind of hero we would admire fully in the tragedies. But the Choruses which celebrate his virtues make perfectly plain that this trim watcher rises from his father's vain engrossing of "cank'red heaps" of gold to genuine magnanimity—the fearless sun king:

A largess universal, like the sun,
His liberal eye doth give to every one,
Thawing cold fear.
(Pro.4.43–45)

A. R. Humphreys: The Style and Its Functions

Those critics who have belittled Part 2 may be suspected of failing to respond to its vitality and maturity of style. Among the aspects of style may be reckoned the interplay of moods and tones. After the urgency of Rumour and the northern nobles, in strenuous verse and tragic tone, Falstaff's wit and foolery are lavish and expansive, quick as the preceding passions but quick with the virtuosity of ease and leisure, elegant wit-patterns contrasting with the thrusting roughness that has preceded them. The comedy of Master Dommelton's reported recalcitrance (which casts Falstaff into a self-appreciative performance of indignation) and of the fencing with the Lord Chief Justice exists in a world antithetical to Northumberland's. The council of war follows, a return to urgent high policy, and then one of Mistress Quickly's great scenes, comic at the most plebeian level so far met in either of the *Henry IV*s. The play extends its scenes and styles to make the widest exploration of the nation's life. London's alleyways in their uproarious disorder form their counterpart to the baronial disorder (and both levels of riot are fated to be quelled by complementary instruments of government, the King's generals, and the King's Justice). This scene (II.i), in boisterous vernacular, forms an offset to the next, that of Hal and Poins at an uneasy loose end, fooling in a restless comedy, somewhat exasperated, somewhat bitter. Critics who think Part 2 to be merely marking time on Part 1 ignore the new elements, of which Hal's restive alienation from his old life is one. In sharp

From "The Style and Its Functions," in The Second Part of King Henry IV, *The Arden Shakespeare* (London: Methuen & Co., Ltd., 1966; Cambridge, Mass.: Harvard University Press, 1966), pp. lxi–lxiv. Copyright © 1966 by Methuen & Co., Ltd. Reprinted by permission of the publishers.

contrast, Lady Percy recreates Hotspur, as a reminder, after Hal's un-
rest, of what the model of chivalry had been.[1] Then follow in succession the tavern scene, as tellingly coarse as anything in Langland or
Hogarth (yet done rather in Chaucer's spirit), an unblinkable indication that Hal must commit himself to a new life; and then the King's
meditation on the revolving times and his own time in particular, a
discourse poetically charged, wholly contrasting with Boar's-Head life,
yet enrichingly juxtaposed with the plebeian state of those over whom,
at the other end of the spectrum, kings rule; and then the switch from
London, whether plebeian or courtly, to Gloucestershire, a part
equally of the King's domain but complementary in spirit and idiom
to the components which have gone before. To pursue the inter-rela-
tionships further would be superfluous save, perhaps, for indicating
the striking force of the scene of Doll's arrest (V.iv), placed between
the anarchistic hopes Falstaff has just voiced and the regal authority
Henry is just about to exert. This inter-animation of successive levels,
speeds, manners, and languages of the play is the more important,
dramatically, in that the narrative content is not greatly compelling.
Much less than in Part 1, or *Richard II*, or *Julius Caesar*, or *Macbeth*,
or *Othello*, does one ask, "What happens next?," though one certainly
asks, "What happens at the coronation?" The play is narrative, certainly, but its dramatic interest is less in narration than in the varying
paces, pressures, and qualities that make the living nation of men. It
is in the manner of writing, the style or styles, that these reveal themselves.

The play has been thought deficient in "poetry," by adherents of
that "lyric heresy" which Lascelles Abercrombie defined as "the doctrine that poetry can only be lyrical; [that] even epics and dramas
. . . can only justify themselves as poetry by their lyrical moments." [2]
This debilitating doctrine can be maintained only by those unwilling
to recognize that "poetry" co-exists with the whole expressive vitality
of language. It is this fuller kind of poetry which *2 Henry IV* abun-
dantly displays. Dr. Tillyard gives the right lead:

> In *Henry IV* there is a variety of style, fully mastered, which is new
> in Shakespeare and which can hardly be matched even in his later work.
> This variety contrasts, and I believe was meant deliberately to con-
> trast, with the comparative monotony of *Richard II*. . . . Taken to-
> gether, the verse and prose of the play are a stylistic exhibition of
> the commonwealth.[3]

[1] Hal, of course, must transcend Hotspur, since Hotspur's valour is anarchic.
But at least he must have Hotspur's virtues (and has, in *Henry V*), of which Lady
Percy's speech is a reminder.
[2] *Theory of Poetry*, New York, 1926, p. 216.
[3] Tillyard, pp. 295–6.

The style, in the first place, expresses great vivacity and manifold energies, observable from the start in the flexible rhetoric of Rumour, engaging the attention by functional changes of direction, rhythm, and stress, reflecting the speaker's heady character in the flux of metaphors, half emerging and then swept out of sight by others:

Upon my tongues continual slanders *ride,*
The which in every language I pronounce,
Stuffing the ears of men with false reports . . .
Whiles the *big year, swoln* with some other grief,
Is thought *with child* by the stern tyrant War,
And no such matter? Rumour is a *pipe*
Blown by surmises, jealousies, conjectures,
And of so easy and so plain a *stop*
That the *blunt monster with uncounted heads*
The *still-discordant wav'ring* multitude,
Can *play* upon it.

This swift generation of metaphors can be studied in the figurative sequence of Morton's speech at I.i.112–25. Here the firing and chilling of spirit, the tempering of metal, and the flight of missiles follow with the swiftest of transitions, so mercurially effected that the mind receives the impress of graphic suggestion without pausing to define the causes, the whole being kept in the plane of suggestiveness (rather than definition) by verbal legerity, almost legerdemain. Such language is vitally metaphorical: it conveys its effects effortlessly but it defies translation into prose. The King's speeches at IV.iv.19–66 evolve with a similar velocity. Such metaphors wed thought and figure intimately—a notable instance occurs at IV.v.98–100:

Stay but a little, for my cloud of dignity
Is held from falling with so weak a wind
That it will quickly drop; my day is dim.

The King's supremacy, overshadowing rather than glorious (and imaged as a cloud), upheld only by his fading breath as a cloud's rain is by gently fluctuating air, will dissolve (a helpless and mournful yielding is appropriate to the King's despondency); his eyesight, life, and reign together are fading. Such is the characteristic metaphorical language of the play.

Chronology of Important Dates

Note: This chronology is reproduced from Eugene M. Waith's in *Shakespeare: The Histories,* in the Twentieth Century Views series, Prentice-Hall, 1965, pp. 180–81, which I saw no need to improve upon. The dates of plays given, as he says, are based on G. E. Bentley, *Shakespeare: A Biographical Handbook* (New Haven: Yale University Press, 1961), and he adds: "Since there is no contemporary record of these performances, the dates should be taken as informed guesses."

1564	Shakespeare born at Stratford-upon-Avon; baptized April 26.
1582	Married to Anne Hathaway.
1583	Susanna born.
1584	The twins, Hamnet and Judith, born.
1590–92	The three parts of HENRY VI performed in London.
1592	First printed reference to Shakespeare in London: Greene's satirical comment on III HENRY VI.
1592–93	RICHARD III, *The Comedy of Errors.*
1593–94	*Titus Andronicus, The Taming of the Shrew.*
1594–95	*Two Gentlemen of Verona, Love's Labour's Lost, Romeo and Juliet.*
1595–96	RICHARD II, *A Midsummer Night's Dream.*
1596–97	KING JOHN, *The Merchant of Venice.*
1597–98	The two parts of HENRY IV.
1598–99	*Much Ado About Nothing,* HENRY V.
1599	Building of the Globe Theater.
1599–1600	*Julius Caesar, Twelfth Night, As You Like It.*
1600–01	*Hamlet, The Merry Wives of Windsor.*
1601	Shakespeare's company hired by followers of Essex to play RICHARD II as propaganda for rebellion.
1601–02	*Troilus and Cressida.*
1602–03	*All's Well that Ends Well.*
1604–05	*Measure for Measure, Othello.*
1605–06	*King Lear, Macbeth.*
1606–07	*Antony and Cleopatra.*
1607–08	*Coriolanus, Timon of Athens.*

1608–09	*Pericles.*
1609–10	*Cymbeline.*
1610–11	*The Winter's Tale.*
1611–12	*The Tempest.*
1612–13	HENRY VIII, *The Two Noble Kinsmen.*
1613	Globe Theater burned down during a performance of HENRY VIII, June 29.
1616	Shakespeare died April 23.
1623	First Folio edition of Shakespeare's plays.

Notes on the Editor and Contributors

DAVID P. YOUNG, editor of this volume, is Assistant Professor of English at Oberlin College. He is the author of *Something of Great Constancy: the Art of "A Midsummer Night's Dream."*

L. C. KNIGHTS is King Edward VII Professor of English Literature at the University of Cambridge, and a Fellow of Queens College, Cambridge. Among his books are *Drama and Society in the Age of Jonson, Explorations: Essays in Literary Criticism, An Approach to Hamlet,* and *Further Explorations.*

CLIFFORD LEECH, Professor of English at the University of Toronto, is the author of many books on drama, including *Shakespeare's Tragedies and Other Studies in Seventeenth Century Drama, Shakespeare: The Chronicles,* and *Twelfth Night and Shakespearian Comedy.* He edited the volume on Marlowe in the Twentieth Century Views series, and is the General Editor of The Revels Plays.

C. L. BARBER, Professor of English at the New York State University, Buffalo, is the author of *Shakespeare's Festive Comedy,* for which he received the George Jean Nathan prize for drama criticism in 1960.

ROBERT B. PIERCE, Assistant Professor of English at Oberlin College, is the author of a forthcoming study of the history plays.

HAROLD E. TOLIVER teaches at the Irvine campus of the University of California and is the author of a recent study of Andrew Marvell.

DEREK TRAVERSI, who has recently held overseas posts in the British Institute and British Council, is the author of *An Approach to Shakespeare* and, most recently, of *Shakespeare: The Roman Plays.*

A. C. BRADLEY spent most of his academic career at Oxford, where he was Professor of Poetry from 1901–06. His classic *Shakespearean Tragedy* appeared in 1904, and the *Oxford Lectures on Poetry,* from which the excerpt in this volume is drawn, five years later.

J. DOVER WILSON was Regius Professor of Rhetoric and English Literature at the University of Edinburgh until his retirement in 1945. He is co-editor of the New Cambridge Shakespeare, and author of such well-known studies as *The Essential Shakespeare* and *What Happens in Hamlet,* and, more recently, *Shakespeare's Happy Comedies* and *Shakespeare's Sonnets.*

E. M. W. TILLYARD, who taught at Cambridge, where he was Master of Jesus College, wrote widely on a number of literary topics. His works on Shakespeare include *The Elizabethan World Picture* and *Shakespeare's Last Plays.*

HAROLD JENKINS, Regius Professor of Rhetoric and English Literature at the University of Edinburgh, is General Editor of the Arden Shakespeare and author of *The Life and Work of Henry Chettle,* and *Edward Benlowes.*

A. P. ROSSITER, who taught at Cambridge and was much admired as a lecturer, was the author of *English Drama from Early Times to the Elizabethans* and *Angel With Horns,* as well as editor of *Woodstock, A Moral History.*

R. J. DORIUS teaches at San Francisco State College and is at work on a study of Shakespeare's histories.

A. R. HUMPHREYS, Professor of English at the University of Leicester, edited both parts of *Henry IV* for the Arden series, and is the author of several books on eighteenth century literature, as well as a study of Melville.

Selected Bibliography

Apart from an attempt to give a clearer idea of the scope of certain works, I have not here listed any of the works included in this collection, nor have I tried to duplicate the references to other criticism made by their authors. The reader's attention is therefore directed to the notes of the above essays and excerpts, and, for further references, to Harold Jenkins' survey of twentieth century scholarship, "Shakespeare's History Plays: 1900–1951," *Shakespeare Survey 6* (1953), 1–15; to the bibliography in Irving Ribner's study (see below under 2); and to Gordon Ross Smith, *A Classified Shakespeare Bibliography, 1936–1958* (University Park, Pa.: Pennsylvania State University Press, 1963).

1. Standard Works on the History Plays

Campbell, Lily B., *Shakespeare's "Histories": Mirrors of Elizabethan Policy*. San Marino, Calif.: Huntington Library, 1947.

Reese, M. M., *The Cease of Majesty*. London: Edward Arnold, 1961.

Tillyard, E. M. W., *Shakespeare's History Plays*. New York: Crowell-Collier & Macmillan, Inc., 1946.

Traversi, Derek, *Shakespeare from* Richard II *to* Henry V. Stanford, Cal.: Stanford University Press, 1957.

2. Works of Related Interest

Charlton, H. B., *Shakespeare, Politics, and Politicians*. The English Association. Pamphlet No. 72, Oxford University Press, 1929.

Lawlor, John, *The Tragic Sense in Shakespeare*. London: Chatto and Windus, Ltd., 1960.

Palmer, John, *Political Characters of Shakespeare*. London: Macmillan & Co., Ltd., 1945.

Ribner, Irving, *The English History Play in the Age of Shakespeare*. Princeton, N.J.: Princeton University Press, 1957.

Schelling, Felix, *The English Chronicle Play.* New York: Crowell-Collier & Macmillan, Inc., 1902.

Spencer, Theodore. *Shakespeare and the Nature of Man.* New York: Crowell-Collier & Macmillan, Inc., 1942.

3. Editions of the Play

The Yale Shakespeare, ed. S. B. Hemingway. New Haven: Yale University Press, 1921.

The Arden Shakespeare, ed. R. P. Cowl. London: Methuen & Co., Ltd., 1923.

New Variorum, ed. M. A. Shaaber. Philadelphia: J. B. Lippincott Co., 1941.

New Clarendon, ed. W. R. Rutland. Oxford: Oxford University Press, 1946.

The New Shakespeare, ed. J. Dover Wilson. Cambridge: Cambridge University Press, 1946.

Pelican Shakespeare, ed. Allan Chester. Baltimore: Penguin Books, Inc., 1957.

Signet Classic Shakespeare, ed. Norman N. Holland. New York: New American Library, 1965.

New Arden, ed. A. R. Humphreys. London: Methuen & Co., Ltd., 1966.

Note: Of the above editions, the New Arden is by far the best. The Pelican and Signet are reliable, inexpensive editions. J. Dover Wilson's edition is full of interest, but the reader should beware of interpolated stage directions designed to support the editor's interpretation of the play.

4. Sources

Bullough, Geoffrey, *Narrative and Dramatic Sources of Shakespeare,* Vol. IV. London: Routledge and Kegan Paul, Ltd., 1960.

5. Articles

Hunter, G. K., "Shakespeare's Politics and the Rejection of Falstaff," *Critical Quarterly,* I (1959), 229–36.

Jorgensen, Paul A., "The 'Dastardly Treachery' of Prince John of Lancaster," *PMLA,* LXXVI (1961), 488–92.

Knights, L. C., "Shakespeare's Politics," *Proceedings of the British Academy,* 1957, pp. 115–32.

Law, R. A., "Structural Unity in the Two Parts of *Henry the Fourth,*" *Studies in Philology,* XXIV (1927), 223ff.

———, "Links between Shakespeare's History Plays," *Studies in Philology*, L (1953), 175–82.

Shaaber, M. A., "The Unity of *Henry IV*," *Joseph Quincy Adams Memorial Studies*. Washington: The Folger Shakespeare Library, 1948.

Spencer, B. T., "2 *Henry IV* and the Theme of Time," *University of Toronto Quarterly*, XIII (July, 1944), 394–99.

Stewart, J. I. M., "The Birth and Death of Falstaff," *Character and Motive in Shakespeare*. London: Longmans, Green & Company, Ltd., 1949, pp. 111–39.

Williams, Philip, "The Birth and Death of Falstaff Reconsidered," *Shakespeare Quarterly*, VIII (1957), 359–65.